Working in the
Commonwealth of Books

Working in the Commonwealth of Books

1960–2025
A Cultural Memoir

Keith Helmuth

Chapel Street Editions

Appreciation of Place

Chapel Street Editions exists within the unceded and unsurrendered territories of the Wolastoqiyik, Mi'kmaq, and Peskotomuhkati people. The work we do is born from the stories carried by this land and its inhabitants. The animals, plants, soil, water, and air make this place home for the Indigenous people who belong to this land, for the descendants of those who took this land and made it a belonging, and for those who have since come from away. Chapel Street Editions holds a deep appreciation for our place within this land and the stories it tells. We honour the land's Indigenous caretakers and are grateful for their wisdom and guidance.

Copyright © 2025 by Keith Helmuth
All rights reserved

Published by
Chapel Street Editions
150 Chapel Street
Woodstock, NB E7M 1H4
www.chapelstreeteditions.com
chapelstreeteditions@gmail.com

ISBN: 978-1-988299-58-7

Library and Archives Canada Cataloguing in Publication

Title: Working in the commonwealth of books : 1960-2025 : a cultural memoir / Keith Helmuth.
Names: Helmuth, Keith, 1937- author
Identifiers: Canadiana 20250205114 | ISBN 9781988299587 (softcover)
Subjects: LCSH: Helmuth, Keith, 1937- | LCSH: Publishers and publishing—Canada—Biography. | LCSH: Book industries and trade—United States. | LCSH: Book industries and trade—Canada. | LCSH: Booksellers and bookselling—United States—Biography. | LCSH: Booksellers and bookselling—Canada—Biography. | LCSH: Academic librarians—United States—Biography. | LCSH: Academic librarians—Canada—Biography. | LCSH: Books and reading—United States. | LCSH: Books and reading—Canada. | LCGFT: Autobiographies.
Classification: LCC Z483.H45 A3 2025 | DDC 070.5092—dc23

The type is set in Iowan Old Style, designed by sign painter and typographer John Downer.

Book design by Brendan Helmuth.

A man ought not to work for any why... but only for that which is his being, his very life within him.

Meister Eckhart

All that I hope to say in books, all that I ever hope to say, is that I love the world.

E. B. White

Previously Published

Tracking Down Ecological Guidance:
Presence, Beauty, Survival

Tappan Adney
and the Heritage of the Saint John River Valley

Arrowhead to Hand Axe:
In Search of Ecological Guidance

If John Woolman Were Among Us:
Reflections on the Ecology of
Flush Toilets and Motor Vehicles

Co-Author

Tappan Adney:
From Birchbark Canoes to Indigenous Rights

Paths of Faith in the Landscape of Science:
Three Quakers Check Their Compass

It's the Economy, Friends:
Understanding the Growth Dilemma

Genetically Modified Crops:
Promises, Perils, and the Need for Public Policy

How On Earth Do We Live Now?
Natural Capital, Deep Ecology, and the Commons

Fuelling Our Future:
A Dialogue about Technology, Ethics,
Public Policy, and Remedial Action

Right Relationship:
Building a Whole Earth Economy

Dedication

For Ellen — forever
and for
Eric & Brendan

Table of Contents

Preface

The composition of this memoir was triggered by my discovery of Joseph A. Michaud's account of "the book trade in and around Iowa City." In 2011, my wife, Ellen, and I were visiting Iowa City after a forty-eight year absence. Iowa Book and Supply was still in business at the same location although the lower level had been completely renovated and expanded. I engaged the bookseller on duty with my nostalgic memories of the store from the late 50s and my history as a bookseller at The Paper Place in Iowa City in the early 60s.

As a good bookseller, he immediately asked, "Do you know Joseph Michaud's book, *Booking in Iowa: The Book Trade In and Around Iowa City, a Look Back*? It has a section on The Paper Place." I did not, but nothing could have interested me more, and I responded accordingly. He took me to the shelf and put the book in my hands.

Back home in Woodstock, New Brunswick, I wrote to Joseph Michaud with information about the origins of The Paper Place and its significance, which was missing from his account. He replied with interest, saying he would add my information if he did a second edition of the book.[1]

What I was inspired to write is the first chapter of my story about working in the commonwealth of books. I shared my narrative with Michael and Marlene Fine who were the original proprietors of The Paper Place and Achilles and Olga Nickles who joined the Fines in the operation of the store. They encouraged me to continue my bookseller's story. I likewise sent it to Dan Traister, a consummate

---

1   After UNESCO named Iowa City a world class *City of Literature*, Joseph Michaud also wrote and published *Iowa City, City of the Book: Writing, Publishing, and the Book Arts in the Heartland* (2011).

bookman and then head of the Rare Book and Manuscript Library of the Van Pelt-Dietrich Library at the University of Pennsylvania, and to Susan Stewart, the Avalon University Professor of the Humanities at Princeton. They both knew something of my story in the book business and encouraged me to continue my memoir.

Once started on this journey of remembrance, the people, places, and events of my years in the book trade, as a librarian, and now as a publisher clamoured for a place on the page. And especially, the books central to this story crowded round for recognition of their of their significance. It all seemed a little daunting, but once started I was able to systematically return to the task, and over the course of ten years bring the tale to completion. A lot of material was left on the cutting room floor, but that is as it should be in crafting a narrative of this kind.

My focus in assembling this story has not been just personal. I call it a "cultural memoir." My various positions in the commonwealth of books over the past sixty-five years enable me to hold a small mirror to this multifaceted era. Books crowd the stage of my presentation and through them a larger story of cultural change, and cultural crisis unfolds.

In the Introduction to the second edition of *Understanding Media*, Marshall McLuhan writes as follows:

> The power of the arts to anticipate future social and technological developments, by a generation and more, has long been recognized. In this century Ezra Pound called the artist "the antennae of the race."

A worker in the commonwealth of books who is attentive to the frontline milieu of the arts, the humanities, the social sciences, and the earth sciences is in an ancillary position for advancing the awareness of how cultural change takes place and what navigating the future will likely require. A lifelong immersion in the world of books and environmental activism has repeatedly put me in this position. *Working in the Commonwealth of Books* is a report on this vocational trajectory.

•   •   •

A variety of references incorporated in this book date to before Ellen and I landed in Iowa City in 1958, and before I started working at The Paper Place. A brief account of our history before coming to Iowa City, what brought us there, and our association with The Religious Society of Friends (Quakers) will provide a bit more background.

Ellen and I met in our junior year at Eastern Mennonite High School in Harrisonburg, Virginia, where I had come from Ohio as a dormitory-student, and where Ellen lived with her family and was a day-student. After graduation in 1955, I completed a year of studies at Eastern Mennonite College (now University)—also in Harrisonburg—before becoming a part-time student at Kent State University near my home in Ohio. Ellen completed two years at Eastern Mennonite College before we were married in 1958.

We came to Iowa City in the fall of 1958 assigned to manage a project sponsored by the Mennonite Board of Missions and Charities. This project provided the opportunity for young men and women to devote two years of voluntary service working as orderlies and nurse's aides in the hospital system of the State University of Iowa (SUI). Near the end of our two years with this project, we resumed our university studies and then stayed in Iowa City to complete undergraduate degrees and take up employment.

The Mennonite Church at that time, while sponsoring charitable work and voluntary, community-based service projects, did not support peace movement activism and generally proscribed political engagement of any kind. With the nuclear arms race in full swing and grade school kids being trained to shelter under their desks in case of nuclear war, that didn't seem right.

I knew from my studies in cultural history that the Quaker movement had been at the forefront of social justice and peace movement activism from its beginning in 17th century England, and that contemporary Quakers carried on the work of this heritage. We began attending the Quaker Meeting in Iowa

City, found a community of like-minded people, and have been associated with The Religious Society of Friends ever since.

Keith Helmuth
Wolastoq Watershed
Woodstock, New Brunswick, Canada
January 2025

Chapter One

What a Kingdom It Was[2]
The Paper Place, Iowa City

I am eternally grateful ... for my knack of finding in great books, some of them very funny books, reason enough to feel honored to be alive, no matter what else might be going on.

Kurt Vonnegut
From a surface plaque on an Iowa City walkway.

Independent bookstores, run by true book people, are unique in the world of commerce. They make a contribution to the social and cultural life of their communities quite unlike any other business operation. Good bookstores are not just purveyors of culture, but actually help generate the lineaments of culture that make the communities they serve rich and satisfying places to live and work. A certain level of conviviality occurs in bars and coffee shops, but the social life of a good bookstore, run by book people, has an ambiance of intellectual stimulation and serendipitous encounter that can often touch the mind and heart in surprisingly significant and long lasting ways.

To speak of "independent" bookstores is, of course, a quite recent bit of nomenclature. Before the rise of Borders, Barnes and Noble, B. Dalton, and — the gods help us — Books-a-Million, all bookstores were proprietorships. Such were the times when The Paper Place opened for business in Iowa City.

---

2   The title of Galway Kinnell's first book of poetry, published in 1960.

Iowa City in the late 1950s and early 1960s was a unique place. It was a city of some 50,000 people, 30,000 of whom were students at the State University of Iowa (SUI). The traditional distinction between "town and gown" in university settings did not apply to Iowa City in those days. It was truly a cultural oasis, characterized by some folks as "Athens in a cornfield." These were the days when we used to say, "Iowa City is the only place worth stopping between New York and San Francisco."

It was the Writers' Workshop that brought Michael and Marlene Fine, the future proprietors of The Paper Place, from New York to Iowa City in 1959. Michael soon saw the opportunity to open a new kind of bookstore—a store stocked entirely with paperback books, hence the name, The Paper Place. In the late winter of 1960 they rented a storefront from Gus Pusateri at 130 South Clinton Street. The location—previously a Mode O'Day women's clothing store—was directly across Clinton Street from Irene Kenny's bar, an old time "watering hole" favoured by writers and artists. Along with several friends, the Fines began to renovate the store for its new incarnation and commenced ordering books. Jim Koller and Dan Gropman built and painted the shelves. Michael began preparing his hand lettered signage for the shelves. With the coming of The Paper Place, South Clinton began to have a somewhat "left bank" aura.

At the same time, Achilles and Olga Nickles had come to Iowa City from New Jersey so he could attend the Writers' Workshop. Achilles, however, was also interested in the bookstore business and noticed what was shaping up at 130 South Clinton. In due course, the Nickles joined the Fines in the operation of The Paper Place. I began working at the store within the first year of its opening and later came to manage it when the ownership changed. Although The Paper Place closed down after a decade of operation, it became a little bookshop with a long legacy. From its early years, it launched the vocational trajectories of three families in the book business that played out for decades to come.

• • •

One day in the spring of 1960, I was walking past 130 South Clinton and noticed the big display window was covered with sheets of brown paper. A sign announced the coming of a new bookstore called "The Paper Place." At that time, Iowa Book and Supply and Hawkeye Bookstore were the only bookstores in town. Hawkeye carried only textbooks and non-book items. Iowa Book was a full service bookstore selling both trade and textbooks. They were also the regional distributor for Doubleday's Anchor books and had a full inventory of this important pioneering paperback line in stock.

Through the late 1950s, I regularly visited Iowa Book's "used and rare" book room on the lower level looking for inexpensive volumes to add to my embryonic and budget constrained library. Though not particularly rare, I did find some gems in that conclave of old books, including an early Everyman Edition of *The Journal of George Fox* and an ancient (undated) edition of *John Woolman's Journal* with a floral design title page reminiscent of William Morris's work, and bearing a quote from Milton: "A Good Book Is The Precious Life-Blood Of A Master Spirit Embalmed & Treasured Upon Purpose To A Life Beyond Life." I also found a beautifully bound and boxed, two volume, Grove Press edition of the Chinese classic, *Shuihu Zhuan* (*Water Margin*), translated by Pearl Buck as *All Men Are Brothers*.

So the prospect of a new bookstore with an offbeat name piqued my interest. I waited eagerly for the opening day. In my late teens I had read Christopher Morley's little classic, *The Haunted Bookshop*, and, behind the brown paper, it seemed to me that sort of imagination-stimulating environment might be taking shape.

Opening day arrived. I probably was not the first customer, but I was surely among the earliest. The unique feature of The Paper Place was immediately apparent on entering the store. The mystery of the name was now revealed. The shelves were stocked entirely with paperback books. The proprietors had brilliantly capitalized on a growing trend in the book industry by opening a bookstore devoted to paperback books.

New American Library had been publishing their Signet Classics mass-market line for some time. Pocket Books had their Washington Square Press line of quality literature. Bantam, Dell, Fawcett, Berkeley, and Ballantine were beginning to release quality books in mass-market editions as well. Penguin Books from England, where quality paperbacks had long been a staple, were now coming into the US market. Lawrence Ferlinghetti had launched City Lights' Pocket Poets Series. Barney Rosset's Grove Press and James Laughlin's New Directions were publishing important new literature directly into paperback. University presses were starting to republish quality literature and scholarly work in paperback editions. Trade publishers were introducing new paperback lines and acquiring important titles in all fields. Harper brought out Torchbooks, Alfred A. Knopf created the Vintage line. Houghton-Mifflin introduced Mariner Books. Viking entered the market with Compass, Harcourt with Harvest, World with Meridian, Doubleday with Anchor. Modestly priced paperback books of serious scholarship and literary value were moving rapidly into the market. A golden age of paperback bookselling was in the offing.

The Paper Place showcased the fact that it was now possible to set up a bookstore stocked with serious literature, high quality non-fiction, and scholarly works all in paperback editions. The university community of Iowa City was the perfect place to launch such a venture. The name conveyed the concept, the image caught on, and The Paper Place became *the* place in Iowa City for good books at low cost. It wasn't the dimly lit, smoke filled environment of Morley's *Haunted Bookshop*, but The Paper Place did have a special ambiance. The dark wood shelving rose to above head height and included an arrangement of alcoves where *spiritus mundi* seemed to me especially present. Michael's hand lettered calligraphy-like signage on the shelves communicated a personal touch. I remember the distinct feeling of coming into the store and feeling in a strange way at "home," of being in a place that particularly suited me. Little did I know what was to come.

The Paper Place became a good deal more than a source for affordable books. It became a place for friendly and stimulating conversation, a place to which poets, short story writers, and novelists who had come to Iowa City for the Writers' Workshop were naturally drawn.

Phillip Roth, who had recently published his first book, *Goodbye Columbus* to considerable acclaim, was on the Workshop teaching staff at this time. He later published a condescending article in *Esquire* on life in Iowa City, but he did manage to say good things about The Paper Place. His second book, a novel titled *Letting Go*, included Iowa City in its long tale of unhappiness and human foibles.

Clark Blaise, who years later returned to direct the Workshop's International Writing Program, was then writing the fine short stories that later appeared in his first book, *A North American Education*. George P. Elliot, already known for his collection of short stories, *Among the Dangs*, was teaching at the Workshop and later helped establish a creative writing program at Syracuse University.

Lucy Warner, who was both a student at SUI and an employee of The Paper Place, published her luminous story, "Other Mornings," in *The Atlantic* during this time. She later published *Mirrors*, a collection of equally fine stories with Knopf. Novelist, Vance Bourjaily, a Workshop teacher and Hemingway-like writer, was a good friend of the store.

Jim Koller, who helped construct the store, went on to create *Coyote's Journal* featuring new American poetry, and to have a series of his own poetry books published over the decades that followed. He left Iowa City before I started working at The Paper Place, but we met years later at Ricker College in Houlton, Maine, where he had come to give a reading. We traded good memories from our respective connections with The Paper Place.

Poetry was serious work for many folks who gravitated to The Paper Place. A ferment of poetry was stirring up new voices on both coasts. Allen Ginsberg had already become famous for *Howl*, and Lawrence Ferlinghetti had launched his flagship book, *A Coney Island of the Mind*. Kenneth Rexroth, who had for years been writing poetry of great cultural depth and transcendent beauty quite outside and beyond the hearing of the literary establishment, had recently begun to host public readings in San Francisco, sometimes with jazz accompaniment. In 1961 *The New York Times Book Review* published his essay, "New Poetry." The essay ends with this self-referencing paragraph:

> Someone once said of one of these older leaders of this new renaissance that he had made poetry a social force in San Francisco. This is about as complimentary a remark as could be made about a poet. Whatever else they have done, our young poets have returned poetry to society. Today in America, more than anywhere else in the world, large numbers of people find poetry interesting. It says something to them, something meaningful in their dilemmas and exultations. This is no small accomplishment.

This renaissance in poetry was not particularly evident at the Iowa Writers' Workshop in those days, but it was percolating around the edges and well represented on the shelves of The Paper Place. I understand a kind of street-level poetry movement did come to Iowa City a few years later. Perhaps The Paper Place helped plant the seeds of this poetic flowering.

My memory is not what it used to be when it comes to names, but I do remember Mark Strand and Marvin Bell from those days. Little did we know the contribution they were to make to our poetic heritage! Donald Justice had been at the Workshop a bit earlier. When his book, *Summer Anniversaries,* was published in the Yale Younger Poet Series, it was a notable book in our Paper Place conversations. His influence had a long lasting effect. I am sure there are other writers equally worthy of note in this story from the early days of The Paper Place that I am simply not remembering.

Entering The Paper Place in those days, you were likely to hear Joan Baez's first album playing in the rear of the store. You were likely to hear it the next day as well. We were all mesmerized. We had never heard a voice quite like this before. Judy Collins had the same effect. Who can forget the first time you heard her rendition of "Both Sides Now"? And then there was Leadbelly and the Weavers and Odette. This rising and enduring folk music helped create the distinct atmosphere of The Paper Place as it charted a unique course in the cultural and commercial life of Iowa City.

While The Paper Place was unique in Iowa City, it had progenitors on both coasts that served as explicit models. Ted and Eli Wilentz had already made 8th Street Bookshop in Greenwich Village a landmark for avant-garde book people in Manhattan. Lawrence Ferlinghetti had not only established City Lights as a mecca for San Francisco's emerging counter-culture, but was also publishing some of the most interesting poetry of the time under the City Lights imprint. Jumping ahead in Iowa City bookstore history, it must surely have been with this heritage in mind that Jim Harris christened his new bookstore, Prairie Lights, in 1978. 8th Street Bookshop is long gone, but City Lights and Prairie Lights carry on.

At some point during the first years of The Paper Place, the second floor of 130 South Clinton became a "coffee house" and a folk music scene called Renaissance Two. I don't recall who the proprietors were, but I do remember the soulful feeling of music from the heart and the delicious taste of hot mulled cider. I remember when Paul Adkins, Jim Hockenhull, and Doyle Moore—known collectively as the Philo Glee and Mandolin Society—came from the University of Illinois and gave a rendition of the old time Appalachian music that was behind the modern bluegrass revival. This was soon after Pete Seeger had been in town for a rousing concert and Ravi Shankar had turned the Memorial Building auditorium into a mesmerizing, incense filled venue for sitar and tabla music.

And there was the literary event that brought Dwight Macdonald, Ralph Ellison, and Norman Mailer together on the same stage for an evening of presentations and conversation on "modern culture." I remember Macdonald saying the problem with *Life Magazine* is that on one page it shows Leonard Bernstein conducting a symphony orchestra and on the next it has a photo of an elephant on roller skates. The general effect is to create the impression that both events are of more-or-less equal importance. I remember Ellison's saying he rather enjoyed the luxury of the Cadillac motorcar, which may have been a riposte to Macdonald's disdain of "masscult." I don't remember anything Mailer said, but then I was focused on what Dwight Macdonald had to say, having recently read his books *The Root is Man* and *Memoirs of a Revolutionist: Essays in Political Criticism*.

Iowa City's reputation for an extraordinary cultural flowering was well deserved. One summer during this time — I think 1961 — the University Theatre staged a Shakespeare Repertoire program. I had read my classroom quota of Shakespeare, but this series of summer productions was an explosion of comprehension and appreciation for me. Indeed, Athens *and* Stratford in a cornfield! Equally memorable and even more powerful were the productions of modern dramas that were regularly staged including Beckett's *Waiting for Godot*, Strindberg's *The Dream Play*, Ionesco's *Rhinoceros*, and Brecht's *Caucasian Chalk Circle*. In addition, there was a small movie theatre that specialized in European films and where we were inducted into the worlds of Bergman, Truffaut, Fellini, De Sica, and others. Many a time, after being carried away, I would walk out of that theatre and have to make an effort to realize, oh, yes, here I am in Iowa City.

About this time something entirely new in the world of commerce and culture appeared in Iowa City. Tom and Marcia Wegman opened a store adjacent to The Paper Place with an intriguing name — Things and Things and Things. Both Tom and Marcia were artists and they filled their emporium with products and artefacts that delighted the senses, augmented wardrobes, and spiced up decor. Later in the 60s, stores like this often became collections of questionable taste and value, but the Wegmans had both taste and style and their store was a hit. They have both gone on to become remarkable artists. With The Paper Place and Things and Things and Things side by side, South Clinton became an even more interesting social and commercial scene.

I was only a modest customer of The Paper Place, but I became a great browser, and in browsing discovered a talent for quickly picking up and remembering titles, authors, and the themes of books — a talent that stood me in good stead for my future career in bookselling. I remember in particular the purchase of Bertrand Russell's *A History of Western Philosophy*, Frazer's *The Golden Bough* and Karl Löwith's *Meaning in History*. I could see the proprietors of this store knew what they were doing when they ordered books. Everything on the shelves appealed to serious readers and inquiring minds. I remember walking back to our apartment at 118 Bloomington and beginning to read Russell's *A History of Western Philosophy* on a hot summer evening with the distinctive smell of the big feed mill south of town wafting in the open window.

In those days I was working part time at the Hospital School for Handicapped Children — a division of the SUI medical school and hospital complex — while my wife Ellen completed her under graduate work at the University. The income from this employment was $100 a month. Our rent was $60 a month. We relied on big boxes of Quaker Oats and ten-cent cans of red beets to stretch our food budget. We had very little for the purchase of books and I mostly used the SUI Library for following out my program of reading and study. (This great library was open twenty-four hours a day, seven days a week, year round — a bibliophile's paradise.) It was, therefore, a memorable day for me when I found the shelves of The Paper Place newly stocked with a selection of Pendle Hill Pamphlets. Pendle Hill is a Quaker study centre near Philadelphia that publishes a pamphlet series on a variety of spiritual, cultural, and broad human concerns of vital import.

These pamphlets not only interested me a great deal, but they fit our budget. They were priced at $.35 to $.70 each. Here I found Lewis Mumford's essay *The Human Way Out* on overcoming the impasse of the Cold War and the nuclear arms race. I picked up Peter Viereck's *Inner Liberty: The Stubborn Grit in the Machine* — a trenchant call for remaining "unadjusted." Equally memorable was finding Simone Weil's lost work, *The Iliad or the Poem of Force*.

First translated by Mary McCarthy, this seminal essay was then published by Dwight Mcdonald in the November 1945 issue of his periodical, *Politics*. Pendle Hill picked it up for their pamphlet series in 1956 and it has been in print ever since. Such are the discoveries that an intelligently stocked bookstore, small though it be, affords the diligent browser. Finding these pamphlets also foreshadowed our future association with the Religious Society of Friends (Quakers).

As I became a regular at The Paper Place, I also became better acquainted with Achilles and Olga and Michael and Marlene. In the spring of 1961 I was again a full time student finishing up the last of my undergraduate studies. I had taken so long many of my friends were graduate students and the difficulties that seemed to dog their climb up the academic ladder had no appeal for me. But I loved the world of books, so one day I asked Achilles if there might be an opportunity to work at The Paper Place.

I remember it so clearly; Achilles was standing at the sales counter on the raised platform near the front of the store. He looked down at me with a quizzical smile and asked in return, "You'd like to work here?" I said, "Yes, I would." We talked a little more and he said he'd let me know. The next time I was in the store he said I could start anytime. I started working part time and on Commencement Day that spring I was on duty at The Paper Place instead of in the Field House for the graduation ceremonies. I had gotten the degree. I didn't need the ceremony. The Paper Place was where I wanted to be. And that's how I got started in the book business.

• • •

In 1962, changes came to The Paper Place. Gerald Stevenson took over the operation of the store. Achilles and Olga returned to New Jersey. Michael and Marlene returned to New York. Gerald Stevenson, at that time, was the head of the Mathematics Library at SUI, and the proprietor of The Qara Press. He certainly was a book person but he was not a business management person. He turned to me for the management of The Paper Place. Gerald and I hit it off immediately, especially when we discovered that not only were we from the same area of northeast Ohio, but that my mother had worked as a housekeeper for the Stevenson family when Gerald was a kid. They both remembered each other.

Gerald and I became great friends. He was an extraordinary character, as is well noted in Joseph Michaud's 2009 book, *Booking in Iowa: The Book Trade in and Around Iowa City, A Look Back*. He was also the soul of generosity. He did a beautiful letterpress announcement for the birth of our first child, Eric, and refused to take anything in payment. He had a great wealth of knowledge about significant but often little known books. He introduced me to *Islandia* by Austin Tappan Wright, a book that has remained a beacon of sanity for me as the ensuing decades have piled up into environmental and social crisis. Gerald put me on to *Eyes of Discovery: America as Seen by the First Explorers* by John Bakeless, *Plants, Man and Life* by Edgar Anderson, *Farmers of Forty Centuries: Permanent Agriculture in China, Korea and Japan* by F. H. King, and *Land and Life* by Carl Ortwin Sauer. These were eye opening and horizon expanding books for me just as my work in history was moving into a study of geography, human settlements, and ecological adaptation.

Gerald was one of those persons who could talk interestingly about almost anything and we had amazing conversations on a wide range of topics. He was a highly social person and a first class raconteur who missed no opportunity to hold court. But, along with the talking, he was also attentive to others and a good listener. The Paper Place was the perfect place for the exercise of such a talent and Gerald loved it. The bookstore drew a wider range of traffic than Kenney's bar across Clinton Street, which had previously been one of Gerald's chief venues for discourse and dialogue. Holding court at the bar often became less and less coherent as the evening rolled along. Holding court at the bookshop, with a coffee pot at the ready, made for a higher quality conversation all around.

I remember one October night in 1962 in particular. Michael Fine was visiting from New York. We were gathered with several friends in the back office listening to the radio and talking intermittently. We were in a somber mood. The Cuban missile crisis was cresting toward catastrophe. The US government's ultimatum to the Soviets was hanging in the air. The Soviet ships, presumably carrying more missiles, were approaching Cuba. The US Navy had set up a blockade.

We kept talking late into the night. Nobody wanted to go home and go to sleep. There was something in the air we had never felt before—the sense that this might be the last night. The movie *On the Beach* had recently been in the local theatre, and now something of this feeling was approaching in real time and real life. The next day, when the Soviet ships turned around and the crisis broke toward survival, the sense of reprieve was palpable. The bookstore had been a good place for sharing thoughts and emotions during that night of great tension and high anxiety.

Gerald Stevenson was part of an Iowa City circle of letterpress artists and fine bookmakers who had been students of master printer Harry Duncan at the University's Typographic Laboratory. This circle included Kimber Merker who succeeded Duncan as Iowa City's master printer with his Stone Wall Press. Kimber eventually founded the University's Center for the Book and its Windhover Press. In 1961 Gerald Stevenson prepared, printed, and published a book that was the masterwork of The Qara Press—*Thomas James Cobden-Sanderson: Selections from His Writings and Including a Portion of an Hitherto Unpublished Notebook*.

Cobden-Sanderson was a printer and bookmaker in late 19th century England, a contemporary and colleague of William Morris. He was responsible for the work of Doves Press during the time when some of the most beautiful books in the history of printing were produced there. Gerald's book was a tribute to this illustrious but difficult artistic ancestor, and was named one of the fifty best books of the year by the American Institute of Graphic Arts in 1962. Gerald was immensely pleased with this recognition of his work.

The Paper Place thus became a crossroads of association for the book arts in Iowa City. Somewhere there is a photograph of

Kimber, Gerald, and I, along with Doyle Moore, who was visiting from the University of Illinois, in front of The Paper Place. We are all fully bearded—an uncommon sight in those days—which had prompted the photographer to take the snap. He said we looked like we belonged on a Smith Brothers Cough Drop box.

Over four decades later in Philadelphia I met Lucy Duncan who had been born in Iowa City the same year as our first son, Eric. She had a complete set of her father's Cummington Press books, all beautifully letterpress printed and hand crafted. As I carefully took each volume off the shelf for a closer look, the days when I was a bookseller among such book artists rose into view, and the title of Galway Kinnell's book from that time—*What a Kingdom It Was*—came to mind. We all have our golden age memories and this is one of mine.

Gerald was always cheerful and almost always whistled as he walked the streets of Iowa City. You could hear him coming half a block away before he burst through the door of the bookstore with an energetic "Good morning," even though it might be early afternoon before he made his appearance. His enthusiasm was infectious. I will never forget his reaction to first reading the title poem of William Stafford's book, *Traveling Through the Dark*, published in 1962. Stafford had graduated from the Writer's Workshop in 1955 and Gerald was eagerly awaiting this publication of his first major collection. A lot of what I came to feel and understand about poetry comes from following him into orbit around that remarkable poem.

Gerald was a great friend and companion, but his attitude toward the responsibilities of proprietorship soon began to trouble me. The workload continued to slide more and more in my direction, and the part that he, as owner, had to do often did not get done. My management of the store did not extend to financial accounting. This was in Gerald's hands and I am sad to say that much slipped through his grasp that needed close attention, including payments to publishers. The Paper Place was flourishing when Gerald took over, but now the stock was thinning out and sales dropping. Publishers shut off shipments. It became clear to me that if I wanted to follow a career in bookselling, this was not the place to be, as much as I liked Gerald, The Paper Place, and Iowa City.

Thanks to Achilles and Olga Nickles, I had an alternative. When they left Iowa City and returned to New Jersey, Achilles told me he and his brother, Peter, would be looking for a place to open a new bookstore, and if I were interested in joining them he would let me know. As it turned out, Achilles and Peter opened two new bookstores at the same time, one in Philadelphia on the campus of the University of Pennsylvania and one in Syracuse on the campus of Syracuse University. We moved to Syracuse in the fall of 1963 and I joined Achilles at the Syracuse Book Center, 113 Marshall Street.

Gerald Stevenson kept The Paper Place going until 1969, but closed the business after a fire and an unsuccessful attempt at relocation. The legacy of bookselling that began with The Paper Place, however, lived on. What started for me with The Paper Place in 1960 continued with the Syracuse Book Center in 1963, and, almost destiny-like, experienced a rebirth thirty-five years later in Philadelphia—a story to which I will return in the penultimate chapter of this memoir. But now it's time for the story of bookselling on Marshall Street in Syracuse in the mid-60s—and what a time it was!

Chapter Two

Bookselling on Marshall Street
Syracuse Book Center, Syracuse

*I have burned ever brighter with a book vending
enthusiasm.*

Mason Locke Weems, 1794-1825
New Jersey book peddler

Few people open shoe stores because they really love shoes, but
book people open bookstores because they really love books, or
more precisely, the world of books, which means literature, history,
art, science, religion, philosophy, poetry, music, communication,
the social sciences, and the whole panorama of human culture
and natural history that is almost magically imprinted on paper
and gathered between the covers of books.

People with an interest in retail enterprise will generally consider the opportunity that various kinds of merchandise offer for
a successful business. People who open bookstores are motivated
the other way around. A life with books, a business in books, the
working day surrounded by books and book people is the appeal,
and the entrepreneurial inclination goes in search of a suitable
setting for this singular vocation.

Such was the case when Achilles and Olga Nickles returned
to New Jersey in 1962 and began the search for a good location
to establish a new bookstore. Their search was for a particular
kind of location, a university setting similar to that of The Paper
Place in Iowa City. The University of Pennsylvania in Philadelphia
was a logical prospect. For one thing, Achilles was a graduate of

this venerable institution; for another, the university community, in 1962, was being served book-wise only by a typical university-run bookstore.

Together with his brother Peter, Achilles researched a number of university settings, and, in the end, also selected Syracuse University as a prime location. In 1963, they opened two new bookstores at the same time. Peter Nickles opened the Penn Book Center at the corner of Walnut and 34th Streets on the campus of the University of Pennsylvania. Achilles and Olga, with two-year old daughter Nina, moved to Syracuse and opened the Syracuse Book Center at 113 Marshall Street on the campus of Syracuse University. Thus began a family enterprise in the book business that lasted until Achilles and Olga retired in 2006.

•   •   •

In 1962, I made a decision against going to graduate school. I had several good friends who were toiling away on graduate degrees and the stress of their situations warned me off embarking on such a course. I had taken seven years to complete a university degree, partly because of having other things to attend to, and partly because I pretty much took only courses that really interested me. The day came when my faculty advisor at the State University of Iowa looked over my record and said; "It looks like you're a history major." I had more credits than needed to fulfill the degree requirement, so it was time to wind things up and assign a category of accomplishment to my efforts. My engagement with university education had been a joy and I was sure I could continue to learn what I wanted to learn without the stress of being jacketed and pummelled by the gatekeepers of graduate degrees. I already had a job I loved in a bookstore and good contacts that might lead further in that career.

When Achilles contacted me in early 1963 with the news that they were opening stores in both Philadelphia and Syracuse, he invited me to join the venture and consider which of the locations we might be interested in. "We" now included son, Eric, born in April of that year. Although I visited the Philadelphia store, there was never really a question about which location to choose. I wanted to work with Achilles. There was something about the way Achilles brought me into the business, something about the way he provided basic training, and something about the way he responded to my ideas and initiative for store development that was very comfortable and would bode well for future teamwork.

When I visited Syracuse in the spring of 1963 to assess the opportunity and to meet again with Achilles before making a decision and coming to a definite agreement, he took me out to dinner at a restaurant where I had the best seafood I had ever eaten. Perhaps it was the momentousness of the occasion that has placed that dinner in my memory in this way. Little did I know what would unfold for our family from the decision in process, but I knew this was an important step. I also remember Achilles asking me what seemed, at the time, a strange question. We were talking over a range of things and during a pause in which I was savouring a bite of delicious fish he asked me if I was an atheist. I wasn't taken aback because we were both serious people and, even though casual, this was a serious question. I said, "No."

I had some years earlier figured out that atheism was not an adequate response to the problem of monotheism. Atheism was just the flip side of a monotheistic mindset that had ceased to believe. The psychology is exactly the same; the certainty of a fixed belief, although opposite, settles the metaphysical question. This seemed to me an unsatisfactory way of thinking about and understanding the great world of Creation and the unaccountable experience we call consciousness.

Having come early in life to an unmistakable sense of presence in the mystery of earth's great commonwealth of life, atheism seemed to me a throwaway category which closes down the kind of openness to the world and experience that makes life's journey really interesting. Imagination and openness to experience is the human forte; it seems a waste to close it down with a clap of certainty in any direction.

I didn't really think of all this before I answered Achilles's question. My "no" came spontaneously from the heart. The question was not the kind you expect in the last stage of an employment arrangement, but it made me feel even warmer toward Achilles. The fact that he valued communication at this level was yet another sign that the social world of the bookstore business was a good place to be. (These were the years of the great "death of God" debate in liberal religion and radical theology and my story of bookselling on Marshall Street will return to this metaphysical theme.)

•   •   •

I found it difficult to tell Gerald Stevenson I was leaving The Paper Place and Iowa City. He was a dear friend but his sense of business protocol was hopelessly deficient. I had the feeling we were sailing into deep water on a sinking ship. Michael and Marlene Fine, who were still partners with Gerald in the ownership of the business, came to Iowa City for a visit that spring. I took the opportunity to fill them in on the state of the operation, and to tell them I was leaving to join Achilles at the Syracuse Book Center. They were taken aback but sympathetic. The news wrought a change in Gerald and he became more attentive to business. But our decision had been made, and by the end of the summer our plans for making the move were complete.

Leaving Iowa City was not easy. We had lived there since 1958 and had many friendships and associations that, had we stayed, would have grown deeper and richer. We were part of the local Quaker meeting that included Manfred and Agnes Kuhn, Bill and Selma Connor, Norvall and Joan Tucker, and Brian and Edith Michner.

Manfred was the founder of the "Iowa school of symbolic interaction" in the field of sociology. He was a much loved and extraordinarily insightful professor at the University. Agnes was a vital activist in the Quaker community. Dr. Bill Connor was a medical researcher with whom Ellen worked on pioneering cholesterol studies at the University Medical Center. Selma frequently hosted the activities of the Quaker Meeting at their home. Norval was a painter and both a professor and administrator in the Art and Art History Department of SUI. Joan and Norval were avid gardeners, which also connected with our interests. Dr. Brian and Edith Michner were elderly and wise Quakers who particularly befriended us as a young family in the Meeting. This association with the Religious Society of Friends, as Quakers are formally known, foreshadows a yet to come turn in my vocation with books.

On learning that we were moving, Mr. Swisher, our elderly landlord and owner of considerable rental property in Iowa City, responded by saying that if we would reconsider he could offer me a position in the property management business. I was touched by his offer, but, for me, the business of property management couldn't hold a candle to the business of bookselling. I had been unpacking those shipments of new books, creating displays, and engaging delighted customers long enough to know that there is a dimension of on-going learning, as well as intellectual rapport and social communion that serendipitously pops up in the book-store business that suited me to a T.

Kimber Merker, master of letterpress bookmaking and the book arts, knew from our conversations that the woodland and mountain environments of childhood and youth figured in our plans to return to the East. He temptingly offered that if we remained in Iowa City, we would be welcome to accompany his family to his wife's family ranch in Montana each summer. That *was* appealing, but it was the eastern woodlands and mountains that held sway in our longing for a more home-like place.

Iowa City was a fine place, but the surrounding countryside was almost nothing but a landscape of farmland. There were woodlots here and there on the farms but often you could see right through them from one side to the other. No mystery of the deep woods, not much wildlife either. Having been imprinted from birth by woodland that stretched for miles from my home and by the presence of woodland wildlife nearby, the Midwest, for all its amazing agricultural productivity, seemed, in some way, an impoverished landscape. I know it does not seem that way to native Midwesterners who naturally see it differently. There is no escaping early imprinting. Moving to Syracuse meant the variegated landscape of upstate New York and the forests and mountains of the Adirondacks were within easy reach.

In August, I loaded up our MG TD with as many of our belongings as I could tuck inside and tie down on the rear luggage rack. Our only significant possession was Ellen's portable Singer sewing machine. I made the long trek to Syracuse where I rented a furnished apartment, stashed the MG in the garage where Achilles and Olga lived, and took the bus back to Iowa City.

A few weeks later, in September, we packed everything remaining in our Volkswagen and set out for our return to the East. "Everything," now included six-month old Eric tucked into a baby seat secured in the middle of the car's back seat and surrounded by bags and boxes and pillows and blankets. On the evening of the first day out, as we approached my sister's home in Goshen, Indiana, we were singing "The Fox Went Out on a Chilly Night." We sang it through once and then again. The second time a surprising thing happened. As we came to the last verse, where you sing, "…and the little ones chewed on the bones-ooooo," and the ooooo is raised into a higher register, a little voice came floating from the back seat with a pitch perfect "ooooo." What a moment! On reflection, I think something then dawned on us in a new way—we were, indeed, a family. A good sign of guidance for a new venture! And Eric, now in his 60s, is a composer, a performing musician, and an acoustic engineer.

•　　•　　•

The campus of Syracuse University sits on the upper slope of a long hill that stretches from East Genesee Street to the vast Morningside Cemetery on the east side of the city of Syracuse. In 1963, Marshall Street bordered the lower edge of the campus proper. Marshall runs the four blocks between South Crouse Avenue and Ostrom Avenue on the western edge of Thornden Park at the top of another hill. The intersection of Marshall and Crouse, and the block running east to University Avenue, was in those days the commercial and social centre of the University campus.

The main "watering hole"—The Orange (named for the University's athletic colors)—was around the corner on Crouse. A Walgreens Drug Store was on the corner of Crouse and Marshall. The other end of the block was anchored by a store called Manny's. Aside from the University Bookstore, Manny's was the only other shop in the area that sold books. But Manny's main business was clothing and other student supplies and paraphernalia. Books were part of the business in the way greeting cards are part of a drug store's business. The lack of a good academic bookstore is what made this university community a prime site for a new store.

This was the setting in which Achilles rented 113 Marshall, just two doors up the block from the corner of Crouse. It was an excellent location with a high level of foot traffic passing up and down the street. One drawback, we discovered, was that the record shop on the west side of Crouse had a big loud speaker mounted outside over the door that played Beatles songs almost non-stop. This was early Beatles, before *Rubber Soul* and *Sgt. Pepper*. "I Wanna Hold Your Hand" seemed to be the record shop's all time favourite and we had to endure its obsessive playing over and over day after day. When *Rubber Soul* was released in 1965, it was clear something had happened to the Beatles. They were now in a different place and headed into new musical territory. Since then, I have been able to hear the early Beatles—even "I Wanna Hold Your Hand"—with a sense of their genius yet to come.

One thirteen Marshall was a typical, single story, flat roof, storefront structure. Although an individual building, it stood wall to wall with its neighbours, as did all the structures along this section of the street. The buildings along Marshall Street presented that variegated range of faces that give older commercial districts a diverse and visually pleasing prospect. The buildings have the appearance of having been built in the 1920s and 1930s. The Varsity Restaurant, reported to be the first Marshall Street business, was established in 1926. It's still in operation.

Our location was well suited for a bookstore. It had a central entrance with two large display windows on either side. The interior was wall-to-wall open space with only two steel posts supporting the roof. A room at the rear, open to the main floor, provided additional display area.

When I arrived, the store had been open for several months. The sidewalls had been fitted with shelving, and three rows of chest high island shelf units were set up running the length of the store. In the back room Achilles had installed a large multi-tier periodical rack and filled it with literary and academic journals, cultural and political magazines, and international newspapers. Perhaps more than anything else, this selection of periodicals gave the Syracuse Book Center its cachet as an academic bookstore, run by people who valued being in touch with the literary, artistic, scientific, political, and cultural currents of the time.

It was at the Syracuse Book Center that I began to work with all the elements of design, layout, organization, and display that became an important source of my job satisfaction in the bookstore business. The Paper Place was completely laid out and furnished with bookcases and shelving when I came into the picture. Its space was small, perhaps six hundred square feet, and no room was left for expansion or redesign. The Syracuse Book Center was considerably larger, probably a thousand or more square feet, and, when I arrived, had yet to be fully fitted with shelves and display units. I immediately saw the opportunities. The whole back wall was a blank slate waiting to be filled with shelving. There was a gap between the bookcases on the east wall and the walk-in window display area that turned out to be just the right amount of room to insert shelves for a poetry section.

A key factor in creating a bookstore that draws its customers into a pattern of frequent visits is a large and continually changing display of new releases. If you are an avid book person, the habit of frequent browsing is strongly reinforced when you know every time you stop by your favourite bookstore you will likely see newly published books in the new release section.

Now, some might say this is just smart marketing and a way to push up sales. Of course it is this, but in the book business it is much more. It is truly a service of the same sort performed by your public library when the staff set out displays of newly arrived books. Readers of literature want to know what's being published and are delighted to find a new novel by a favourite writer. Scholars are always on the lookout for new works in their fields of study and research. Poets are keen to see what their compatriots in the craft are up to from season to season.

So we set about devoting significant space to the display of new releases. I built a three-sided unit around the structural post at the front of the store, which was the first thing you saw when you entered the front door. On the immediate right a five shelf unit eight feet long was devoted to new releases, and to the left, running the length of the slightly elevated order service and sales desk, I set up a narrow table that displayed two rows of new books.

I admit, this was a little like those displays of candy bars that grocery stores and pharmacies set up at the check-out counters. But in my defense, I can argue that books don't pile on calories making you overweight, or bathe your teeth in cavity-producing sugar. Picking up an extra book that you hadn't come to purchase, but, having found, can't resist, won't go amiss. I know it's playing to an "addiction," but at least it's not a sugar addiction.[3]

My prime confirmation for making this "information service" a major feature of the Syracuse Book Center was the number of times customers would exclaim something like, "Oh, I am so glad to see this." One of the main things customers watched for was the release in paperback of a book they had held off purchasing in hardback.

· · ·

These were the days when the format known as the "mass-market" paperback was rapidly shifting to include quality literature and even academic and scholarly works. Popular fiction, mysteries,

---

3   There is a Japanese expression for this habit. "Tsundoku (n.)
    The constant act of buying books, but never reading them.
    Specifically, letting books pile up in one's room so much that
    the owner never gets a chance to read all of them. Japanese
    slang from 'tsunde-oku' (to pile things up for later) and
    'dokusho' (reading books).

westerns, and science fiction, with a light sprinkling of non-fiction and classic literature had been the stock-in-trade of mass-market book publishing since the 1930s. Priced at 25 and 35 cents, these small format, small print, paper editions made books more widely available than ever before.

By the early 1960s a shift was well underway that included not only an upgrading and expansion of books selected for publication in mass-market editions, but a definite improvement in design, paper quality, and durability of binding. This new generation of mass-market books had upgraded pricing as well, ranging from 50 to 75 to a top of 95 cents. Mass-market publishers were now paying huge sums for the rights to reprint highly successful new books, and, with the price under a dollar, were banking on selling a ton of copies in order to make a profit. This was getting dicey and the big question in the industry was this; could mass-market publishers break the $1.00 price barrier without hurting sales?

When the big test came, it was a non-fiction book that blazed the pricing trail beyond the $1.00 ceiling. *The Rise and Fall of the Third Reich* by William Shirer had been published in 1960 to popular acclaim and academic controversy, which, of course, made it even better known and sought after. It was a ponderous book of over 1200 pages. Within a couple of years the hardback sales had tapered off enough to start rumours about a paperback edition — a mass-market paperback edition, no less. A book this size challenged the $1.00 price barrier *and* the problem of a mass-market binding adequate to the dimensions of over 1200 pages. Nothing like this had been done before.

Publisher's Weekly kept us informed on the rumours and the bidding for publication rights. Finally, it was announced that Fawcett Publications had purchased the paperback rights to *Rise and Fall of the Third Reich* for an enormous sum — $100,000. This was unheard of; it was way beyond the norm. Fawcett announced they were working on the binding problem and would release the book with a price of $1.75. There was a kind of gasp and then a wave of scepticism about this price that made its way through the trade. Not only was Fawcett breaking the $1.00 barrier, they were plunging deeply into untried pricing territory. Many folks thought it was a big gamble, considering this was a history book of massive size, and not a best selling novel. Considering what they had paid for the rights, they obviously were hoping to make the project pay off.

And pay off it did! I well remember the day our shipment came in. I don't remember for sure the quantity we ordered, but my guess is probably 50 copies, which is a lot for any new book. We unpacked them, stacked them up near the front of the store, and proceeded to ring up the sales. The $1.75 seemed to make no difference. For those who wanted the book, and had held off on the hardback, this was a bargain. It's true, it was a mass-market format, but at something like 3 inches thick it sure didn't look like a mass-market book. And the binding was a success. It was flexible and could be opened for easy reading without cracking. The $1.00 price barrier had been smashed and shortly thereafter pricing for more normally sized mass-market books began to move up from $1.25 to $1.45. William McNeil's masterwork, *The Rise of the West: A History of the Human Community* — also a hefty book — was priced at $1.50 and sold well.

The movement of popular hardback books into paperback during this time came to have an almost chronological predictability. You could figure on just about a year, give or take a few months. But if sales of the hardback were holding up well, the paperback could be delayed. *Publisher's Weekly* was our faithful guide to what was coming when. New books were announced well in advance of publication, and release in paperback was tracked well in advance as well.

Publisher's Weekly was my main tool for letting customers know what was coming and how long they would have to wait for the paperback edition. We also had that wonderful reference tool, R.W. Bowker's *Books in Print*. If memory serves, it was during these years that *Books in Print* went from a two to a three-volume set, issued annually. With the paperback boom, the world of book publishing was fast expanding. Bowker responded by publishing a separate *Paperbacks in Print* and issued periodic supplements during the course of the year. In the age of the internet, we may think, "how primitive," but it was a good system and served us well in responding to customer inquiries.

•   •   •

With an increasing number of paperback books becoming available from the regular trade houses, university presses, and from a growing number of small presses, I drew up a plan to substantially increase our stocking capacity. The three rows of island shelf units that ran the length of the store were only chest high, and so, like a good urban planner, I could visualize the value of the space above the current structures. Out came the graph paper, the ruler, yardstick, and the sharpened pencils.

With a little drafting work I soon had my plans for another story of shelves rising on the foundation of the present fixtures. I worked it out so my construction would add three more shelves on both sides of each unit. Moving from the graph paper and pencils to the tape measure, saw, hammer, nails, screws, screwdriver, brackets, T-square, level, glue, clamps, shims, many board feet of good pine lumber and a few sheets of plywood, I went to work, mostly after hours at night and on Sundays, turning my plans into a satisfying reality. When the project was completed we had added two thirds again as much stocking capacity to the three central island fixtures of the store.

Our storefront had two large display windows. Behind one window a raised platform made a good space for creating various kinds of book displays, sometimes of new books, sometimes of books on a theme. The space behind the other window was occupied by another raised platform that accommodated the sales and special order counter, plus a small office space.

I was at first in a quandary over how to make good use of this window for book display. Then one day it hit me: A vertical shadow box unit built to fill the whole window top to bottom and side to side would do the trick. I made it with adjustable shelves between the uprights to accommodate different size books. When it was done I had a unit that could display up to forty books, each in its own open box section. It was the perfect design solution for that space. As the eye scanned the display from the outside, each book stood out quite distinctly. Many were the times when working at the special order desk I would glance up to find several people standing in front of the window systematically scanning from book to book.

•　•　•

In addition to creating more space for books, we made display room for a few select non-book items appropriate to an academic bookstore. Achilles was a skilled player of the ancient Asian game of Go, so, along with elegant and unusual chess sets, we stocked several sizes of Go boards and the accompanying stones. This ancient game, originating in China over 2500 years ago, became known in Europe in the late 19th century and was introduced to North America by Edward Lasker who founded the New York Go Club in 1905. Go is an "encircling game" requiring a talent for strategic, spatial thinking. According to chess master Emanuel Lasker: "The rules of Go are so elegant, organic, and rigorously logical that if intelligent life forms exist elsewhere in the universe, they almost certainly play Go."

So among the things I learned from Achilles in the book business was how to play the game of Go. On evenings when we were both in the store with no pressing office work and a light flow of customers, Achilles would get out the Go board and attempt to initiate me into the logic of the game. Although he patiently taught me the basics of the game, I must admit I did not take to it the way he did and never became a proficient player. I did learn this, however; there are different kinds of visualization and visual memory. I couldn't plot my way through a well thought out strategy on the Go board, but I could see in detail the construction of my second story shelf units before they were built. Diversity makes good teamwork.

Achilles also had a strong appreciation for the visual arts and added an inventory of high quality, matted reproductions of great paintings and drawings. I remember, in particular, the drawings of Kaethe Kollwitz, which were new to me at the time. When Brendan, our second son, was born in 1964, I purchased the famous Kollwitz drawing, "Child in Arms," It has been a presence in our family ever since.

Along with the prints, Achilles brought in a selection of Caedmon spoken word LP records, including several Dylan Thomas albums. I had for some time been moving into a deeper appreciation of poetry, but when I heard these Dylan Thomas recordings for the first time, I was catapulted into a realm of poetic cadence and resonance from which I have never returned.

Achilles added an unusual touch of the fine arts to the décor of the Syracuse Book Center. High on the back wall, above the bookshelves, he mounted a large reproduction of Hieronymus Bosch's masterwork — *The Garden of Earthly Delights.* This triptych, with the dawn of Creation in the Garden of Eden on the right, the large centre panel crowded with the delights (so-called) of earthly living, and the left panel crammed with the miseries of Hell, is not so much a biblical theme as it is a field of play for fantastic imaginings and masterly painting.

This was a complex and sombre artefact to display where everyone who came in the store was sure to see it — hardly normal décor for a retail business. It was, I think, a signal that this shop was not a normal retail business. This was a bookstore, and a good bookstore has a mission for advancing the elements of culture that stir the imagination and spur the mind in its quest for meaning.

I know this sounds overblown. The Syracuse Book Center was just another business on the commercial strip of a mid-sized university. But it's not overblown and I can say why. Hardly a day went by without stimulating conversation with customers, or between customers. The literature, history, science, art, philosophy, religion, politics, economics, anthropology, and humour (yes, we had a humour section) of the world was spread out around us and people who came into the store were generally engaged with the world in a questing kind of way. Minds and imaginations met in the Book Center, and the work of engagement with the elements of culture was advanced again and again.

• • •

The Book Center kept evening hours, staying open until 10 p.m. In those days, in that university community, people were out and about on Marshall Street, and the evening trade was a good part of the business day. Evening hours encourage browsing. After the workday or the day of classes, folks often go out for dinner or a drink. Stopping to look at the display of new books in our window was a common activity. The browser may then step in to see if the new issue of *Commentary* or *Encounter* or *Dissent* has arrived, or to pick up a reserved airmail copy of the *Guardian* at the front desk. Then a close look at the new release section would be in order.

Browsing takes many forms, but its characteristic is always leisure. A bookstore with evening hours affords the browser the opportunity to exercise a talent for leisure, and, as German philosopher Josef Pieper so clearly explains in his gem of a book, *Leisure, The Basis of Culture*, leisure is just that—*the basis of culture*. And, of course, browsing frequently leads to the delightful experience of finding a book you didn't know you needed. That's a win-win for both bookstore and customer. Reciprocity strikes again!

There is another kind of reciprocity that pops up in the bookstore business. Customers will often let you know when you are out of a title they expected to find, or they may recommend a title the store hasn't carried but which they regard as worthy of consideration. This latter interaction with customers, especially in a university community where both faculty and graduate students are doing research, is often an important path of discovery for the bookseller.

Conversations with professors and graduate students about their reading and research can alert you to not only individual books but to clusters of books in a particular field that are getting special attention at the institution to which you are attached as a bookseller. The Book Center cultivated a strong special order service and the incoming flow of these requests was an important checkpoint for learning about the research interests of our scholarly customers and a window on the intellectual and cultural currents afloat in the community at large.

A good example of this is the way the work of Marshall McLuhan came to my attention before he became a cultural icon. One of our best customers, Rob Morrison, was a strange character who did not fit the scholarly stereotype but was clearly and passionately engaged with philosophy and culture, and embarked on a quest to understand and make sense of what was going on and what it all might possibly mean. He was a tall, gaunt fellow, probably in his 40s who would have looked at home on a factory floor. As I recall, he had a teaching position at a nearby college, but had also attached himself to the university community, and particularly to the Book Center. He ordered a continual stream of books to follow out his studies and was also working on a philosophical manuscript made up of both poetry and prose meditations, a kind of Whitmanesque work.

Rob was an intense character, eager to talk about his studies and his writing. When he special ordered *The Guttenberg Galaxy: The Making of Typographic Man* by Marshall McLuhan, which had just been published by the University of Toronto Press in 1962, I took a close look at it and ordered another copy for myself. McLuhan had previously published *The Mechanical Bride: The Folklore of Industrial Man* (1951), a mind-bending look at advertising and popular culture in general. With the publication of *Understanding Media: The Extensions of Man* in 1964, McLuhan shot into prominence in both the world of popular culture and communication scholarship. *The Guttenberg Galaxy* was the book in between and the *sine qua non* for understanding the historical and cultural analysis that stood behind his view of what was happening in the world and where the metamorphosis of communication and cultural life was likely headed. I added *The Guttenberg Galaxy* to our small selection of hardback books.

Having *The Guttenberg Galaxy* in stock gave me a critical background volume to hand sell when *Understanding Media* brought McLuhan wide attention and he began making the intellectual waves that stirred up controversy in the academy. Beyond this,

McLuhan's work clued me in to that of his mentor, Harold Innis, an economic historian who, in a study with the unlikely title, *The Fur Trade in Canada* (1930), began an analysis of cultural change and communication that led to his classic works, *Empire and Communications* (1950) and *The Bias of Communication* (1951).

These works by Harold Innis figure critically in McLuhan's development, and in the way he placed the modes of communication and associated technologies at the centre of cultural change. All this is a good example of the way a customer's interest and book ordering initiative can lead to the expansion of a bookseller's awareness, and thus to an upgrade in the stimulation factor of a bookshop's inventory. Paying close attention to what customers are reading, and especially what they are ordering, is a prime focus for augmenting inventory. This is a top priority for a bookstore serving an academic community, but good practice for any community-based bookstore.

●   ●   ●

One of the reasons this was a golden age for bookselling was that books were the frontline of intellectual exploration and ferment. We eagerly waited for the next books by certain writers and scholars to see where their creativity and scholarly exploration was headed. Publication in periodicals often foreshadowed the books, but it was in the new books being published that the intellectual ferment of the time was fully unfolded.

For example, it was at this time that books were being written and published on the "death of God" debate. John A. T. Robinson, Bishop of Woolwich, had published a little book titled *Honest to God* (1963) that soulfully explained why even an Anglican bishop might find that intellectual and spiritual integrity required him to abandon the conventional constructions of Christian theology. It became a best-seller. At the same time a radical theologian, Thomas Altizer, began writing and talking openly about the "death of God" and what this meant for religion and spirituality in the modern world. Other theologians and cultural analysts joined the fray. *The Death of God Debate* (1967), edited by Jackson

Lee Ice and John J. Carey, brought together a range of scholars now probing the implications of Nietzsche's infamous declaration and why it was re-emerging in contemporary culture.

At the local level we had a notable scholar at Syracuse University who weighed in on the controversy. Gabriel Vahanian published *The Death of God: The Culture of Our Post-Christian Era* in 1961 and *No Other God* in 1964. He was not a proponent of the "death of God" theology as was Altizer, but was more interested in how this current of thought and exposition had come to be, and what it revealed about the state of culture in our time.

The problem, in a nutshell, was not that militant atheists were attacking Christian theology (that would come much later with Richard Dawkins, Christopher Hitchens, and Sam Harris), but that many people of a more-or-less religious bent were finding conventional theological constructions and explanations losing their credibility; it was not that they were rejecting belief, belief was just fading. Those like Robinson, Altizer, Vahanian, and others were at pains to understand what was happening in the world of faith as it was being subsumed into the cultural currents of the time. That's a bit more than a "nutshell," but it was my take on the dialogue as I ordered, sold, and read the books rising to this cultural crisis in religious life.

Among the other intellectual currents contemporary to the time, and that literally populated the Syracuse Book Center, the work and persons of Stanley Diamond, Thomas Szasz, and Ernest Becker are especially good case studies. Each of these scholars was a serious critic of certain aspects of contemporary society, and for good reason. It's no exaggeration to say that in the early 1960s a long-building sense was coming to a head that modern civilization was going off the rails with regard to healthy social relations and the kind of cultural development that advances human wellbeing.

From Lewis Mumford's magisterial historical analysis of technology and culture, culminating in *The City in History* and *The Myth of the Machine,* to Paul Goodman's trenchant description of the social conditions of youth in *Growing Up Absurd,* to Allen

Ginsberg's *Howl*, which had been launched into the world of poetic literature like a bombshell, to Rachel Carson's ominous warning on environmental deterioration in *Silent Spring*, to Jules Henry's case against the major institutions of modern civilization in *Culture Against Man*, it was increasingly clear that human wellbeing was ill-served by the market-driven march of the industrial-consumer economy.

Similar analysis and critiques were emerging in Canada, the UK, and in Europe: for example *Lament for a Nation* by George Grant, *The Politics of Experience* by R.D. Laing, *Society of the Spectacle* by Guy Debord, and *The Technological Society* by Jacques Ellul. The tenor of all this was that if industrial-consumer civilization continues on its present course, economic fragility, environmental deterioration, and societal dysfunction would increase.

No one was yet using the language of collapse, as is now common among serious scholars of culture, economics, and earth system science, but the implication was clear. Given the increasingly chaotic and precarious conditions of the human situation, the analysts and critics of the 1960s were not wrong in their assessments. But even in their prescient wisdom they did not imagine the level of economic and power inequity, the scale of conflict in social relations, the level of psychic imbalance and emotional dysfunction, or the nightmare of ecological catastrophe into which the wealth seeking of hyper-industrialization and the economics of unlimited consumption has now plunged human societies worldwide. But all of this was in the air and was bubbling up in a ferment of discontent and even outrage at what Henry Miller characterized as "the air-conditioned nightmare." Syracuse University, like virtually all other such institutions around the country, harboured both faculty and students who were seriously engaging with this multifaceted cultural crisis.

Stanley Diamond was an anthropologist who first studied literature before turning to the larger questions of societal structure, human development, racism, and injustice. He was a leading figure in the movement that brought anthropology from the ivory tower of research to an engagement with the real problems of contemporary human societies and the injustices being perpetuated by power and economic inequities.

This was, in addition, a time when the US war in Vietnam was being ramped up on false pretenses and to no good end that could be foreseen. Stanley Diamond, along with many other professionals from various disciplines mounted a powerful opposition to the madness of this war. His time at Syracuse University was brief (1963-1966), but he generated a keen following among graduate students who were also determined to relate their studies and research to understanding and addressing the violence, racism, and injustices of our society.

Perhaps because he had a background in literature and was also a poet, Stanley Diamond worked from a deeper and more fully rounded assessment of the human situation than was typical of the social sciences. Like his mentors, Paul Radin in *The World of Primitive Man* and Franz Boas in *The Mind of Primitive Man*, Stanley Diamond saw the expressions of human cultural development and adaptation that preceded the so-called higher civilizations, and in some cases continued to run parallel to them, as significant repositories of high value relationships for human flourishing. In 1964, he published *Primitive Views of the World*, a collection of essays by colleagues to which he also made a major contribution. In 1974, he published a volume of his own studies titled, *In Search of the Primitive: A Critique of Civilization*.

In 1966, Stanley Diamond started the anthropology program at The New School for Social Research in Manhattan and subsequently developed it into a full department. He created the journal *Dialectical Anthropology*, which provided a publication venue for activist anthropologists. His leadership in this area of professional development was emerging during his years at Syracuse University and the opportunity to attend his seminars and workshops was a benefit of being a bookseller to the academic community that surrounded him. Although I had chosen not to go to graduate school, I was following out my own program of studies in anthropology, and this brief association with Stanley Diamond and the orientation of his work was a valuable opportunity.

Dr. Szasz was an altogether different case. When I landed at the Syracuse Book Center in 1963, he was already causing waves in the psychiatric profession, of which he was a bona fide member. He was also a faculty member at the New York Upstate Medical University adjacent to Syracuse University.

By character and conviction a libertarian, Dr. Szasz saw the freedom and autonomy of psychiatric patients increasingly compromised by the diagnostic medicalization of their behaviour problems and by the coercive manipulation of treatment, including the administration of drugs under the rubric of therapy. With his distinctly humanistic values, he took strong exception to the medicalization of human behaviour that deviated from the prescribed norms.

In my quest to understand human behaviour and its problems, I had started my university work in the field of psychology so I was intrigued by what I was hearing of Dr. Szasz's opposition to what was happening in his profession. Achilles clued me in and introduced me to both Dr. Szasz's book, *The Myth of Mental Illness*, which had been published in 1961, and the author himself, who was a regular customer of the Book Center.

I learned *The Myth of Mental Illness* was soon to be released in a paperback edition. The hardback had sold moderately well, and the notoriety it had garnered made the release of the lower priced paperback edition like a second coming—a circumstance to which an alert bookseller pays special attention.

The stance Dr. Szasz had taken against not only coercive psychiatry but against what he called "the therapeutic state" gave the book a dimension of political relevance that resonated on both ends of the political spectrum. Right-wing libertarians as well as left-wing anarchists were drawn to his analysis. The Syracuse Book Center had customers who styled themselves in each of these cultural camps, and they quickly depleted our initial order of the paperback edition of *The Myth of Mental Illness*. Dr. Szasz paid close attention to how his book was selling so a quick call to Harper & Row for a rush shipment prevented the embarrassment of being out of stock.

Dr. Szasz did not ignore the fact that disturbed brain physiology can cause problematic behaviour, and that such cases need to be understood in terms of brain disease. It was the broad brush of "mental illness" being used to categorize troublesome behaviour and deprive people of both autonomy and responsibility that he argued was an abuse of psychiatric practice. He did not deny the efficacy of psychiatric counselling. He argued that it should be used as a way to help people solve life problems that were making them dysfunctional rather than saddle them with a metaphorical illness that further cripples self-esteem, autonomy, and responsibility.

Dr. Szasz insisted he was not anti-psychiatry, which was also a movement of the time, but simply wanted the practice to be honest, objective, non-coercive, and a firm defender of human rights and personal autonomy. He went on to produce book after book developing the implications of his views for professional, legal, political, and societal development. Although his mainstream colleagues roundly criticized him, he remained a professor of psychiatry at the New York Upstate Medical University and we continued to benefit from his intellectual vitality at the Syracuse Book Center.

•   •   •

Of all the scholars and authors I have come to know in the course of my bookselling career, Ernest Becker has had the most significant impact on my understanding of the human dilemma. Ernest Becker published his second book, *The Birth and Death of Meaning*, in 1962, the year before I became the manager of Syracuse Book Center. He received his PhD in cultural anthropology from Syracuse University in 1960 and remained there in teaching capacities for several years. *The Birth and Death of Meaning: An Interdisciplinary Perspective on the Problem of Man* garnered accolades in a certain part of the social science community, so I knew the book before I met the author.

I hadn't long to wait. Ernest and his wife Marie returned from a sojourn in Italy in 1964 and he was thereafter a frequent customer of the Syracuse Book Center. In particular, he came in to order a regular stream of books for his research. There is no better way for a bookseller to get acquainted with customers from academia than to show an interest in their research. With Ernest's work I didn't just *show* an interest, I *had* an interest since its various themes and concerns coincided to a large extent with my own. But, in addition, I quickly saw that a great deal could be learned from conversations with him and horizons opened that I had not yet explored; Ernest was 40, I was 27.

Ernest's first book, *Zen: A Rational Critique*, had been published in 1961. By 1964 it was no longer in print and I wondered why. I had previously enjoyed a period of study in the East Asian Studies program at the State University of Iowa, which included particular attention to the transmission of Indian Buddhism into China and the influence of Taoism in its transformation into Chan Buddhism, or what came to be called Zen Buddhism when it moved into Japan.

The subtitle of Ernest's book intrigued me. I asked him about the book and why it was no longer available. He told me he had prohibited its reprinting because he was now embarrassed by it. He said it was not so much the content or the analysis but the tone he had taken in writing it that now made him wish for it to disappear from circulation. Here, in this self-criticism, is one of the characteristics that made Ernest Becker an unusual and enormously appealing scholar and teacher. *His work and life describe a trajectory of continuous self-critique and openness to learning.* As he refined and deepened his analysis of the "human problem," and moved from book to book, he was never reluctant to point out the shortcomings in his previous thinking and understanding.

In a certain sense, Ernest was devoted to the tradition of the Enlightenment, but the progressive thrust of its anthropology was deeply tempered in him by his own experience. As an American infantryman in World War Two he had participated in the liberation of Nazi death camps. Even as we held our Enlightenment-like conversations, the American war in Vietnam was ramping up in increasingly sickening ways. The evil consequences of human behaviour seemed an endless historical parade that gave the lie to the Enlightenment vision. This was the conundrum into which Ernest Becker, at this time, was moving with all the intellectual honesty, analytic intuition, and profound concern for humanity that was central to his character and commitment.

Becker's grounding in cultural anthropology was the platform from which he saw the potential for bringing together and articulating a new interdisciplinary construct he called a "science of man." Reaching back to Vico's (1725) prescient *New Science*, moving through the rich and various ranges of Enlightenment observation and social thought, delving into the existential terror of Kierkegaard, incorporating and moving beyond Darwin, Marx, and Freud, pondering the brilliant sociology of Max Scheler, the psychodynamic insights of Otto Rank, the pragmatic realism of William James and John Dewey, and the depth theology of Paul Tillich, Ernest Becker developed a synthesis of social psychology and human social and cultural development that had not previously been achieved. This is only a short list of the intellectual and analytic heritage of which Ernest was a master and on which he drew to chart a new understanding of the "human problem."

As I continued to order books for him, I could see the range of disciplines he was incorporating in his study and could anticipate new books I knew would interest him. He was delighted to find books arriving at our store that he had not been aware of but were germane to his work. One evening he came into the store while I was busy with a customer and began browsing through the history section. I hadn't seen him for a week. When I was free, I greeted him and said, "What kick are you on now, Ernie?" He looked down at me (he was tall), put his hand on my shoulder, and said, "Keith, I don't go on kicks." Fair enough, I had spoken carelessly and needed the reprimand to bring our conversation back to an appropriate level. After his death, I wrote to Marie with this little story. It so well illustrates the seriousness with which he regarded his work.

In 1964, he published *Revolution in Psychiatry: The New Understanding of Man* in which he develops a post-Freudian understanding of the functioning and malfunctioning of human beings. He showed why "mental illness" cannot be defined as simply a medical problem, but is also often bound up with the entire scope of personal development within a social and cultural context.

Much to our loss in Syracuse, but to Ernest's professional gain, he secured a teaching position at the University of California at Berkeley in 1965. This was right in the middle of the Anti-Vietnam War and Free Speech movements, which turned into a student uprising that threatened the authoritarian structure of the University. Ernest was on the side of the students who were demanding curriculum and administrative changes. His appointment was not renewed.

Two thousand students signed a petition for his retention. When University administrators rejected their demand, they proposed that student funding could pay his salary. The University agreed, but said his course would be non-credit. The students said, fine, he's a great teacher; we'll take the course anyway. As much as Ernest appreciated the support, he opted to accept a position at San Francisco State University where S. I. Hayakawa had become president. Hayakawa, following Alfred Korzbski, had helped establish the field of General Semantics in communication and media studies, a movement of frontline scholarship and cultural analysis with which Ernest had an affinity.

Three years later, SFSU blew up in student protest and the occupation of buildings. Hayakawa called in the National Guard and the campus became an armed camp of authoritarian oppression. This was not an educational environment that Ernest could accommodate. In 1969 he was recruited to an interdisciplinary program at Simon Fraser University in Vancouver, where he happily spent the rest of his working life.

Out of all this social upheaval and professional turmoil, Ernest Becker produced one of the best books on education I have ever read. *Beyond Alienation: A Philosophy of Education for the Crisis of Democracy* was released in 1967. Seven years earlier, Paul Goodman had published *Growing Up Absurd: The Problems of Youth in the Organized Society*, a book that helped galvanize the movement for alternative education environments relevant to the lives and full human development of students and teachers alike. *Beyond Alienation* extended the analysis and prescription into the world of higher education.

In 1968, Ernest published *The Structure of Evil: An Essay on the Unification of the Science of Man,* a book on which he had been working for a number of years going back to his time in Syracuse. I was aware of this long gestation because the first time I saw Paul Tillich's three-volume *Systematic Theology* was when we ordered it for Ernest at the Syracuse Book Center. I was curious how theology fit into his research and queried him when he picked up the Tillich books. This was the beginning of a series of conversations that previewed the organization of thought articulated in *The Structure of Evil.* Tillich shows up in an important way in this book.

Following this major synthesis of his scholarship, Ernest collected six essays that buttress the trajectory of his cultural analysis and in 1969 published them under the title *Angel in Armor: A Post-Freudian Perspective on the Nature of Man.*

Then, in 1973, came the book that is built on all his previous work and lays out a fully rounded articulation of the "human problem." *The Denial of Death* is a book that opens a door in the mind that cannot thereafter be closed. This is partly because the explanatory power of his central analysis, when you see it, becomes transparently obvious, and partly because Ernest Becker is such a master of intellectual history and cultural narratives that his synthesis of them into a coherent story of human development is particularly convincing.

The Denial of Death articulates a highly cogent paradigm, a lens of depth perception, as it were, about why and how humans both individually and in groups get themselves into such severe and often lethal conflict with each other and with the environments of earth. His insight into the psycho-dynamics of the denial of death and the cultural systems—symbolic and material—that are erected to enact this denial sets Becker's work in a class by itself. A whole field of research, aptly named "terror management theory," has emerged from Becker's scholarship and the Ernest Becker Foundation has been established to support and advance the significance of his contribution to the human sciences.

The *Denial of Death* was widely reviewed and highly praised. He was pleased but also wistful that he would not be here to participate in the dialogue the book was generating. He died from cancer two months after it was awarded the 1974 Pulitzer Prize.

Somewhere in his writing — I can't at the moment put my finger on it — Ernest Becker says that one of the unique things about our time is that we can now talk seriously about religion in a scientific book. He goes further; he argues that you can't have a credible "science of man" — we would say science of the human — without including religion. And this is what he comes to at the end of his work; while religion is one of the constructs that has been built up within the denial of death and the quest to assert cultural domination, and has, therefore, often fallen into evil ways, it also has the potential for opening into a dimension of experience simultaneously cosmic and terrestrial that may enable humans both personally and as organized societies to abandon the cultural armour, which is the cause of so much conflict, aggression, violence, and oppression.

When he died at age 49, the manuscript for another book — *Escape from Evil* — had been put away. He considered it not fully polished and at the end he had no energy for further work. It's true, it's not fully polished, but fortunately Marie made sure the book was published after his death because she knew Ernest would not want his final assessment to remain unknown.

•   •   •

The blow that fell across America on the afternoon of November 22, 1963, brought everything to a standstill on Marshall Street in Syracuse. It was a Friday afternoon with many people about. But then the motion of the street went quiet, with small groups stopped in conversation. Achilles had just gone out on errands, but quickly returned with the news — President Kennedy had been shot in Dallas.

We had a radio in the Book Center and turned it on. People from the street—many of them regular customers—came into the store. We stood in silence listening to reports as they came in. The information about the condition of the President was increasingly dire, but so much remained uncertain. Some folks drifted out, a few more came in. We were all huddled at the front of the store around the radio in stunned disbelief.

Finally, as the reporters kept repeating what they knew and it was evident no additional information would be immediately forthcoming, folks began to quietly disperse. We closed the store and agreed to remain closed on Saturday. The weekend was spent trying to absorb the shock of what had happened. Little did we know that with the killing of JFK, and the forthcoming assassinations of Martin Luther King and Robert Kennedy, an American political and social nightmare, from which there seems to be no recovery, had descended on the nation.

•   •   •

No account of life on Marshall Street during the early 60s would be complete without a soulful nod to Delmore Schwartz who was, at the time, teaching in the English Department and in the Creative Writing Program that had just been initiated at the University. I was well acquainted with and greatly admired his book of selected poems, *Summer Knowledge*, but I didn't know he was also highly regarded for his short story writing. Achilles pointed me to his early collection of stories, *In Dreams Begin Responsibilities*, which had been republished by New Directions. The title alone is enough to make you want to pick up the book, and the writing, with its poetic cadence, fulfills the expectations aroused by the title.

Delmore Schwartz was a regular customer of the Syracuse Book Center. He was not a browser, as were many other regular customers. He was a special-order customer, and, from the nature of books he was steadily ordering, it was apparent he was deeply interested in the history of art and of painting in particular. I never managed to develop much of a conversational relationship with him even though I would ask him questions about the artists when he picked up the books that had come in. The one memorable conversation I had with him was about how Governor Nelson Rockefeller was to blame for certain misfortunes in his life. It sounded plausible to me. He often came by in the late afternoon on his way to The Orange around the corner on Crouse Street where he regularly "held court" with students and colleagues.

I was a bit taken aback the first time I saw him. After he had picked up a book and left the store, Achilles told me, "That was Delmore Schwartz." He had the unkempt appearance of a man down-on-his-luck. He seemed verbally reticent, and in a general way appeared unwell. He looked like a man in his late sixties, but, as I later discovered, he was in his late forties.

As time went on, he failed to pick up the books he had ordered, even though repeatedly notified of their arrival. Then he would appear, looking the worse for wear, pick up the books, charge them to his account, and order additional books. The payments on the account dwindled as the charges mounted. Achilles was in a quandary about what to do. His appearances continued to be erratic and we heard the same report from his classes.

Eventually, we learned he had gone to New York City, was more-or-less out of touch, and had become a regular at White Horse Tavern in the same way Dylan Thomas had over a decade earlier. This was an ominous echo of an end in the making. It all seemed so sad, but, on reflection, we had seen it coming. He died alone in his room in the Chelsea Hotel in 1965 at age fifty-two. What a loss! Just think what might have been added to our literary and cultural heritage had he lived longer! Delmore Schwartz was one of most gifted poets and short story writers of our time, but, in addition, he had a philosophical turn of mind that gave his work a quality of reflective depth that makes it timeless. His death brought up the same feeling of lament that came to me on receiving the news of Albert Camus' death at age 46 in 1960. I reread *Summer Knowledge* in the same way I reread the books of Camus.

• • •

By 1963, the Civil Rights Movement had become an entrenched force for social change. The "Freedom Vote" campaign had been staged in Mississippi in the summer of '63. The "Mississippi Summer Project," which became known as "Freedom Summer," was gearing up for 1964. Students from Syracuse University signed up to participate in these historic efforts.

When the students returned from the South in the fall of '64, a veteran of the Civil Rights Movement, Rudy Lombard, also came to Syracuse to begin work on a graduate degree. Rudy had been a leader in the sit-ins to integrate lunch counters in New Orleans in 1960 when the movement first started. He had been subject to harrowing experiences at the hands of the police, anti-integration mobs, and arrested.

We knew none of this when Achilles hired Rudy for part time work at the Book Center. We saw him as a personable, soft-spoken graduate student who was willing to reliably take the evening shift behind the sales counter. Only gradually, through conversation, did we come to know the story of his civil rights activism. Rudy never pushed his story forward, but when he could tell I was genuinely interested in the Civil Rights Movement and in what it had already accomplished and was attempting to further accomplish, he was willing, in a modest way, to share the accounts of his frontline experiences.

I had been following the news reports of the Civil Rights Movement and of the violent aggression the white southern establishment was using in an attempt to suppress it. But to hear firsthand about police brutality, about hiding in a tree overnight while the sheriff and his henchmen searched the area for you, and of the fear and hatred expressed by white supremacist street mobs was an unforgettable window into the courage of heart and soul that Rudy and his compatriots brought to their non-violent battle for civil rights and human decency.

When the Civil Rights Movement entered its direct confrontation and non-violent civil disobedience phase, the Gandhian tradition was the obvious moral and strategic precedent. But added to this, and perhaps even more deeply motivating, was Martin Luther King's profound grasp and articulation of Gospel morality: eschew violence, return good for evil, love your enemies, turn the other cheek—hard teachings, no doubt. But they were morally empowering and strategically effective in the context of the social and political milieu of the time and the kinds of changes being worked for.

Stanley Diamond, in discussions of all this, added another level of analysis to the dynamics of the Civil Rights Movement. He observed that the Black communities had a long-standing strategy for dealing with White domination, a strategy he called "patterned evasion." While the expression is self-explanatory, it opens the door to a subtlety of understanding that adds a unique cultural resonance to the dynamics of the Movement's strategy.

When Stanley offered this observation, Rudy took immediate note. He typically took his time to mull things over before contributing to a dialogue, but this observation made immediate sense to him. While the Gandhian tradition was a historically validated strategic component and Gospel morality was heartfelt, a long practice of "patterned evasion" gave the Civil Rights Movement a kind of bred-in-the-bone cultural intelligence that made for endurance.

Rudy Lombard did his PhD in Urban Planning, returned to New Orleans, and spent his life in service to his community, which included co-authoring a cookbook documenting the fact that the Creole cuisine for which New Orleans is famous emanates almost entirely from the skills of Black chefs (*Creole Feast: Fifteen Master Chefs of New Orleans Reveal Their Secrets* by Nathaniel Burton and Rudy Lombard: Random House, 1978).

In his last years, he devoted his energy to organizing and conducting health fairs oriented toward Black men. At his passing, those who knew him well commented on the passion he always brought to the various causes to which he had devoted his life.

My association with Rudy Lombard was relatively brief, but there is something about the conversations we engaged in when we were both on the evening shift at the Book Center that has stayed with me in an indelible way. Things like this happen in bookstores. There is something about people who are drawn to books and who gravitate to bookstores that generates an especially sympathetic resonance of communication.

• • •

These were the years when the persistent enlargement of America's war in Vietnam met with increasing opposition at home. On university campuses, it took the form of the anti-war teach-ins which were often set up to disrupt the normal academic routine with extra-curricular workshops, seminars, and lectures designed to tell the truth about the war and galvanize increased opposition. Among the notable people brought to Syracuse University within this context, two in particular stand out for me — Paul Goodman and Herbert Marcuse.

Marty Eisenberg introduced me to the work of Paul Goodman. He had come to the University of Iowa from New York to do a master's degree in political science. We had become good friends from his frequenting The Paper Place and our ensuing conversations. His master's thesis was on the anarchism of Paul Goodman. *Growing Up Absurd* had just been published and a second edition of a 1947 book Goodman wrote with his brother, Percival, had been published at the same time. This book, *Communitas: Means of Livelihood and Ways of Life*, interested me more than *Growing Up Absurd*, although it was this latter book that was making Paul Goodman famous and, at long last, was to provide a significant income for him from writing and eventually from public lectures.

Two books on education, *Community of Scholars* and *Compulsory Mis-Education*, soon followed, both of which placed him in the forefront of counterculture thinking and the alternative education movement. Paul Goodman pitched in on the anti-war protests and supported the young men who were burning their draft cards, but his concerns were far wider. He held out for a social revolution in which the values of human development, creativity, community based enterprise, and community decision making replaced institutional processing, vocational straightjacketing, the centralized management of the bureaucratic state, and the domination of society by wealth and power seeking corporations.

So, when he was invited to make a presentation by the teach-in leaders at Syracuse University, it was not just for a rally or an afternoon seminar, it was for a full evening held in the School of Forestry's large auditorium. The place was packed. When Paul Goodman walked on stage, he seemed a little taken aback. He told us he had been travelling a good deal of late, but generally meeting with smaller groups in less formal settings. What he did next was remarkable; he took a chair from behind the lecture stand, carried it to the edge of the stage, sat down and began to talk about what he had been hearing and learning from the many student groups he had been meeting with around the country. He talked a little about his ideas connected with what he was hearing, but mostly about why he was encouraged by the readiness of students, and youth in general, to say this system is not working for them, and by the openness he was finding to different ways of education, learning, and vocational exploration, and to different ways of setting up and working out social and economic relationships.

Considering the size of the assembly, the evening took on a re-markably conversational tone. Rising from his chair and walking along the edge of the stage, Paul Goodman encouraged questions, entertained comments, and often, instead of simply answering in the manner of an "expert," added to the question and turned it back to the audience, or provided an observation on a comment that invited further exploration.

At first, it seemed odd; we had come to hear Paul Goodman and glean the wisdom his analysis and the discernment he had to offer. But, instead, he was inverting the traditional speaker/audience dynamic and making us help him do the thinking; he was practicing the pedagogic exercise he clearly and consistently articulated in *Community of Scholars* and *Compulsory Mis-Education*. Those who came expecting an ex-cathedra performance may have been disappointed, but as the evening progressed, it became clear Paul Goodman was not interested in flights of abstraction; he was obviously committed to the immediate and concrete dynamics of this dialogue opportunity. He was a practitioner of collaborative learning.

•　•　•

During these years, it was dawning on many of us that the war system was not an aberration, but was instead an integral part of the American political economy, an economy organized more and more around corporate wealth seeking, geopolitical domination, and, as President Eisenhower warned, the military-industrial complex. The great forerunner of this awakening was C. Wright Mills. With publication of *The Power Elite* in 1956, he placed an analysis of the United States' permanent war economy into the middle of American sociology. It altered the field of study in a way that gave it an increasingly relevant engagement with the larger issues of political economy, democracy, and societal development. In an earlier book, *White Collar: American Middle Classes* (1951), Mills provided an account of how the core of American society was being molded into a passive component of the bureaucratically controlled industrial-consumer economy. Along with David Riesman's book, *The Lonely Crowd* (1950), *White Collar* began a critique of industrial-consumer society that gave sociology a new orientation.

In 1958, Mills published *The Causes of World War Three,* a book written for a popular audience that held the power elite responsible for the permanent war economy. In 1959, he published *The Sociological Imagination*, a book that was essentially Mills' manifesto for the deep engagement of the field in the work of social change and human betterment. It was a book that caught the imagination of scholars, students, and social change activists alike. While *White Collar* and *The Power Elite* were always on face out display, and sold steadily at the Syracuse Book Center in the early 60s, *The Sociological Imagination* outsold them probably two to one. It's a manual for critical thinking, the kind of book that turns on a new light, and articulates a new paradigm of analysis and discernment.

In 1964, Herbert Marcuse published *One-Dimensional Man,* which immediately became another flagship book of the era. By this time, the Book Center was ordering and selling more and more newly published hardback books. The anticipation of new books by certain authors made the sales of these more expensive books a sure thing. Marcuse had published *Eros and Civilization: A Philosophical Inquiry into Freud* in 1955, a book that had grown in reputation and was a steady seller at the Book Center. *One-Dimensional Man* had a ready audience waiting for its publication.

The book strikes a familiar but updated theme presented within a historical and philosophical context of which Marcuse is a master. He details the advance of the militarized, industrial-consumer economy and the way it is flattening both personal life and societal functioning into a one-dimensional perspective that is more and more manipulated by the power elite for their purposes and benefit. This sabotaging of personal vitality, progressive societal development, and the authentic processes of democracy was a matter Marcuse took to heart and on which he was eager to take an activist teaching role.

Although he left Germany in 1933 and immigrated to the US in 1934, his earlier association with The Institute for Social Research (The Frankfurt School) and the studies he had done in collaboration with its leading figures gave Marcuse's work the unmistakable aura of the politically engaged analysis and critical depth of European social philosophy. In the same way he had drawn on Freud without being a Freudian when writing *Eros and Civilization,* he drew on Marx without being a Marxist in the composition of *One-Dimensional Man.* Like Murray Bookchin, who was beginning to demonstrate a superlative talent for historical narrative and forward looking syncretic analysis, Marcuse was also enormously appealing to the youth movement of the early 60s. Independent thinking, not beholden to ideology, was the *sine qua non* for fruitful dialogue and sympathetic collaboration in those days. Herbert Marcuse, like C. Wright Mills, Paul Goodman, and Murray Bookchin, was a strong-minded thinker who did not hesitate to lay out his best analysis, but then picked up the dialogue to open further exploration.

I read *One-Dimensional Man* before reading *Eros and Civilization*. It was Ernest Becker who urged me to read both *Eros and Civilization* (1955) and Norman O. Brown's *Life Against Death: A Psychoanalytic Interpretation of History* (1960). Both books had been published before I entered the world of bookselling and I had missed picking up on their significance. Marcuse's book was published the year I graduated from high school and had discovered Thoreau. By the time Brown's book was published, I had done the reading in Freud that was required by the interdisciplinary Humanities Program at the State University of Iowa, and that was enough for me.

I appreciated that Freud was a breakthrough thinker for the culture of which he was a prime example, but I was by this time reading widely in anthropology, comparative cultural history, geography, and the environmental sciences. Given this opening horizon of studies and the realities of human adaptation to earth's various environments and its resources, the Freudian worldview, and the cultural tradition of which it is a part, seemed to me like an exotic hothouse that exaggerates certain aspects of human functioning in the service of aggrandizement—aggrandizement that works both positively and negatively. On the one hand, there's a metaphysical inflation of the human to just "a little lower than the angels," and on the other a glorification of aggression, violence, domination, and war. Something is definitely wrong with a cultural tradition that combines such lofty metaphysics with such horrible behaviour and considers it "normal," the best we can do. I often remember a comment Alan Pistorious, a fellow student at SUI, made about why he was taking Professor William Aydelotte's Modern European Intellectual History class at SUI; he explained he was trying to understand the "European charnel house."

What I didn't appreciate until I read both Marcuse's and Brown's books is that their takes on what Freud had wrought are attempts to construct an understanding of what in the world is going on with human development—at least in Western Civilization—that it so often burns out in grandiosity or sinks into miserable dysfunction. So Freud seen through the reworking of Marcuse and Brown was enlightening, especially since they were not content to let Freud's pessimism have the last word. Both men, and both books, pull out of Freud's end-of-life nosedive into fatalistic resignation and offer a potential alternative for human development and societal advancement. This is what made both *Eros and Civilization* and *Life Against Death* flagship books for those who were now rising up in cultural opposition to business as usual in education and its relationship to the military-industrial complex and the permanent war economy.

So having backed up and read *Eros and Civilization* after reading *One-Dimensional Man*, I was pleased to get the notice that Herbert Marcuse was coming to Syracuse University as part of the anti-war teach-in program. He was scheduled for a full evening address and discussion. However, when I checked my calendar, I discovered to my dismay the Marcuse event was scheduled for the same night as the last in a series of Charlie Chaplin films. What to do? I had attended all the previous screenings in the series and I didn't want to miss the final one. Yet, attending a Marcuse lecture was a significant opportunity that might not come my way again. I had to choose between an evening devoted to art or politics, aesthetics or ethics. I chose for art, only to discover the film was Chaplin's serious spoof of Hitler, *The Great Dictator*. My evening turned out to be an amalgam of art and politics, aesthetics and ethics.

In 1965, Marcuse published *A Critique of Pure Tolerance*, in which he combined with Barrington Moore Jr. and Robert Paul Wolf to explain why the liberal ideal of tolerance, if taken as an absolute, clears the road for the return of repression at the hands of those opposed to the full flourishing of democracy. This is a tricky problem, but one that cannot be avoided. In this tract for the times, Marcuse and colleagues unpacked this paradox as well as they could. I have found it bears rereading and has lost none of its frontline relevance.

•   •   •

In 1961, Barney Rosset at Grove Press took the plunge and published the first American edition of Henry Miller's, *Tropic of Cancer*. It had been originally published in Paris in 1934 by Obelisk Press but banned in the United States ever since. As the owner and publisher at Grove Press, he figured it was time to break the ban and did so by taking the legal case that was brought against him all the way to the US Supreme Court and, in 1964, winning. Up to that point, the Grove Press edition remained in hardback, which somewhat limited its circulation. But before the Supreme Court's decision was handed down on a five to four vote, the word came that Grove had a mass-market paperback edition in the works.

Although devoted to literature and the role of the bookstore in literary life and intellectual culture, Achilles was cautious and prudent in his approach to business. When the release date of the paperback edition of *Tropic of Cancer* was announced, we had to make a decision about whether to order the book, and, if so, how many copies. The "whether" decision hinged on the possibility of being charged by local officials for selling a book still legally banned in the US. The "how many" decision, if we decided to go for it, hinged on our estimate of the number of copies we were likely to sell in the first rush of demand when the $.75 edition was stacked up on the new release display table.

We calculated the risk of being arrested and charged was low since it was well known that the case was headed to the Supreme Court. In addition, the Syracuse Book Center was located on the campus of Syracuse University, some distance from the commercial district of the city. We had already been carrying *Tropic of Cancer* in our small inventory of hardback books. It was unlikely the Syracuse Police Department would act on their own initiative, or that anyone in the community was likely to lay a complaint requiring the police to act.

With that settled, we turned to the question of how many copies to order. Achilles tended to be cautious with numbers. Being the owner of the business, it was his job to manage the cash flow. Being the manager of the floor and book buyer, it was my job to manage the sales flow. When a popular book is about to be released in paperback, and I knew there would be a demand from people who have been waiting for the less costly edition, the trick is to order enough copies to carry an inventory through the first rush. If you run out while the rush is on, sales will go elsewhere, except for those loyal customers who are really attached to the store and are willing to wait for their copy. In addition, you run the risk of a re-order being met with an "out of stock" reply from the publisher and having to wait until a new printing has come in and is eventually shipped to fill your order. Precious days and even weeks can elapse until your new supply arrives, by which time the bloom may have gone off the rush.

When we pre-ordered *The Rise and Fall of the Third Reich*, as earlier recounted, I stretched to fifty copies and hit it just about right. Sales slowed down before we ran out and a reorder came promptly to keep our supply constant. So, how far should we stretch with *Tropic of Cancer*? Achilles said how about seventy-five or maybe one hundred. I said let's do one hundred and fifty and he said OK. It was the right call. Each day as the stack of books diminished we could generously resupply knowing we had a deep inventory yet to go. By the time the sales rush slacked off we still had a small inventory and could now reorder in smaller amounts to meet the continuing, though lesser, demand. Such are the small satisfactions of estimating your bookstore's market reach and making a judgment call that gets it right on a best-seller.

I first encountered the writing of Henry Miller when I picked *Big Sur and the Oranges of Hieronymus Bosch* off the new acquisitions shelf in the lobby of the library at the State University of Iowa. What a strange title and what a weirdly illustrated dust jacket — a Big Sur coastline scene with figures from *The Garden of Earthly Delights* dancing on the beach. I knew nothing of the writer or the painting that was referenced and reproduced inside, but a quick perusal of the book and its section of photographs from the Big Sur coastline and landscape made me want to read it.

I had been to California on a family trip and had spent time in the San Francisco area. I had recently read *The Holy Barbarians* by

Lawrence Lipton, published in 1959, and was mildly gripped by the California counter-culture mystique. I was sympathetic to the Beatnik ethos, but I was not a city person. Squalor and high-risk living had no appeal for me. But here was Henry Miller, clearly an elder paragon of the counter-culture, living with great simplicity in an environment of surpassing beauty. The book spoke to me. I checked it out and thus began my reading of Henry Miller before *Tropic of Cancer* and *Tropic of Capricorn* made their appearances in American publishing.

Fortunately, James Laughlin, the founder of New Directions, had the good sense to publish Miller's various collections of essays and memoirs after he returned to the US from France where he had been living and from Greece to which he travelled on the way home. Since I was already a "bookman," Miller's memoir, *The Books in My Life*, drew me in like a magnet. What a treat! I was introduced to a whole bevy of writers and books I had not yet encountered, some obscure and idiosyncratic but often much to my taste. Kenneth Rexroth's book, *The Classics Revisited*, which I later discovered, had much the same effect on me.

Next came *The Air-Conditioned Nightmare*, a collection of essays occasioned by Miller's return to the United States in 1940. The title has become a meme. People now use it with no attribution and without knowing who coined the expression. I think Miller would be pleased. He had a knack for this kind of phrase. Before he left for Europe Miller worked at Western Union, which in *Tropic of Capricorn* he renamed the Cosmo-Demonic Telegraph Company. The next two books of essays were titled *The Cosmological Eye* and *Remember to Remember*, then *The Wisdom of the Heart,* and a memoir of his time and travels in Greece, *The Colossus of Maroussi*—often referenced as his best book from the standpoint of a coherent and focused narrative. I have a special fondness for *The Wisdom of the Heart* because I was reading it and had it in my coat pocket while I waited to be told I could join Ellen in her hospital room to greet our second son. I had recently read the Penguin edition of *The Voyage of St. Brendan*. We liked the name Brendan and gave it to this new member of our family.

Miller's book length essay on Rimbaud, *The Time of the Assassins*, has a special place in my memory as well. Sometime after reading it, I was taking Ralph Freedman's European Literature course at the State University of Iowa. A course requirement was to produce a substantial paper on a writer of our choosing from the syllabus. Professor Freedman was a great teacher and I wanted to do something that pleased him. I wrote a paper about Rimbaud under the influence of Henry Miller about which Freedman had a wry comment.

In no way did I copy or plagiarize Miller's work. My paper was very unlike what Miller had written. What reading his book had done was show me a way of writing about literature and literary figures that cut loose from the boilerplate of literary criticism and expressed from the heart what one feels about the significance of a writer and their work. Ever since I had read Thoreau in my second year at university, I had a reference point of critique with regard to societal development, political economy, and the human-earth relationship—in a word, culture—that came to structure almost all the papers I subsequently wrote for course assignments no matter the subject. I had a point of view and it worked. It worked to get me started with the writing and worked to carry me through to the end. I said to myself, what would Thoreau say, and I was off and running.

A paper about Rimbaud was a good fit for this method and I had Henry Miller's example behind me to give it a shot. Professor Freedman gave me an A minus on the paper. In commenting on it when I met with him, he said my paper wasn't so much about Rimbaud and his poetry as it was about my worldview. But, he said, it was a lively, impassioned essay, and a pleasure to read. Ralph Freedman later went to Princeton and wrote wonderful biographical studies of Rilke and Hesse.

•　　•　　•

Herman Hesse brings me back to the Syracuse Book Center. Another of James Laughlin's prescient decisions was to publish Hesse's book *Siddhartha*, an account of a man's life that closely parallels that of the one who became Gautama Buddha, but also differs in important ways. To say the book became a cult-like classic is an understatement. Hesse was famous in North America for this one book, but he had written many other novels. In the early 60s the only other of Hesse's books published in the US were *Steppenwolf, Magister Ludi,* and *Journey to the East.* I did some research and discovered that Peter Owen, Ltd in England had published five additional Hesse novels in modestly price hardback editions: *The Prodigy, Demian, Gertrude, Goldmund* (retitled *Narziss and Goldmund* in a later American edition), and *Peter Camenzind.* I did the calculations, including shipping costs, and figured it would not only be a profit making move but a bit of a coup for the Syracuse Book Center to import a supply of these otherwise unavailable Hesse titles. I consulted with Achilles and placed an order for ten copies of each title. When they came in I displayed them in the window, placed them on the shelf in the German Literature section, and watched the inventory melt away into the hands of delighted customers. I placed another order and kept the books in stock thereafter.

The poetry section in most bookstores — if they even have one — is often an anaemic afterthought. As much as I value the work of poets, I have to admit that in building up the shelf capacity and enlarging the inventory of the Syracuse Book Center, poetry was given short shrift until the other categories of mainstream academic and literary interest were fully stocked. Meanwhile, the poetry section got shifted hither and yon to wherever a little extra shelf space remained or opened up.

Finally, after I was satisfied that the prime categories of the most sought after books were well accommodated and displayed, I began looking around for a place to install a decent poetry section. All the regular wall space was filled. We had gone as high with the island fixtures as was reasonable. I then spotted an irregular area of wall between the vertical end of the Literature section and the window platform, which was backed by the New Release shelf unit. If I slid the New Release section closer to the front entrance, it would create access to that as yet unused wall space.

A nice set of five shelves could be custom built to fit the area and, voilà, we would have a poetry section of generous size right up front, which could also be plainly seen from the front window. When I moved the poetry books to their new abode, the space was commodious enough that many titles could be displayed face out. Low and behold, we then found our modest supply of poetry books dwindling day by day. High visibility and face out display is a key to selling books, even, or perhaps especially, poetry books.

Syracuse University had recently established a Creative Writing Program and the Book Center was a favourite haunt for both students and faculty. It was evident our now prominent poetry section was getting attention. Seeing the opportunity, I pulled a selection of publisher's catalogues from my file and systematically assembled orders that would begin to fill up the five shelves. New Directions poetry books were at the top of my list along with City Lights Pocket Poet Series. I turned to the Yale Younger Poets Series and the Wesleyan University Press Poetry Series. I had been collecting the catalogues of a variety of small presses, many of which featured the work of contemporary poets. It was here, distributed by the Four Seasons Foundation, that I found Gary Snyder's first book, *Rip Rap*, printed in Japan with a traditional hand-sewn binding. His second book, *Myths & Texts*, was available from Corinth Books.

I made sure the poets of the modern cannon—American, English and European—were well represented as well and finished off the bottom shelf with a wide-ranging selection of anthologies. As new poetry books came in, I displayed them front and centre on the platform behind our big window that faced directly onto the sidewalk. The attention to our poetry section continued to increase, as did the sales. Rather than being low on the inventory-monitoring list, as was previously the case, the poetry section now rose up the ranks. There's nothing like increasing sales to command attention. It was easy to keep my eye on the poetry section because it was adjacent to the new release section, which I attended to almost daily. Inventory control was entirely a matter of eye, brain, and clipboard—an analog system that keeps you on your toes and generally gives you an 80 to 90 percent success rate when a customer asks, "Do you have..."?

A little later, Gary Snyder was on a poetry reading tour and Cazenovia College, twelve miles southeast of Syracuse, was on the agenda. I had been reading and recommending his books so the opportunity to meet him was timely. He was travelling light. In addition to his ordinary clothes, he wore a long cloth folded in a roll and tied around his waist in which he carried his travelling essentials, one of which I noticed was the Athenaeum paperback edition of *Tristes Tropiques* by Claude Lévi-Strauss. What a great book to read while on extended travel—compact in size, nearly 400 pages in length, and printed in vanishingly small type, as was often the case in those days. He explained that this rolled and folded cloth, tied around the waist, was a traditional Japanese mode of carrying your travel goods.

After his reading we talked a little anthropology. At the time, I was reading Clark Wissler's 1926 book, *The Relation of Nature to Man in Aboriginal America*, which made an interesting counterpoint to the Lévi-Strauss book. Later, I sent him a note about Stanley Diamond's book, *Primitive Views of the World*. It turned out he had met Diamond and already had the book. He said he was working on an essay titled "Poetry and the Primitive" and would send me a copy when it was finished, which he thought might be in six months. I received it two years later, which I thought was pretty good timing. Some time after that, in an exchange of correspondence on common interests, he wrote, "we have been drinking from the same springs."

•   •   •

Among the book culture promotion projects I hatched for the Syracuse Book Center was the writing and publishing of the *Book Center Review*. About once a month I would write several reviews of newly arrived books of interest to the academic community we served. I would add a list of other new books in stock and books scheduled for release in the near future. Our New Release section was a big set of shelves and it sold a lot of books. I cut the stencils for the *Review* on my Olivetti typewriter and ran off copies on the mimeograph machine set up in the store's basement among the backstock shelves. I would then make the rounds of all the departmental offices in the humanities, arts, and social sciences — the areas of the Book Center's forte — placing the Review in faculty mailboxes. We put a stack on a table by the door for customers to pick up as well.

Two of my reviews garnered unforeseen attention, one promptly and one several years later. In 1965, Pantheon Books published Jan Myrdal's *Report from a Chinese Village*. The book received a lot of attention partly because the author was the son of Gunnar and Alva Myrdal who had co-authored *The American Dilemma: The Negro Problem and Modern Democracy* (1940), a classic study based on their extensive socioeconomic research at the end of the Great Depression. The other reason was that Jan Myrdal was objectively sympathetic to the collective social and economic arrangements of the village where he lived for two months while conducting extensive interviews with its residents. The Chinese government had never before allowed a journalist to conduct this kind of research on the effects of the Revolution. Myrdal didn't gloss over the hardships or down-play the failures, but on the whole his report indicated that the village was coping with their social and economic conditions in positive, progressive, and hopeful ways.

The book was unusual because it was the first fact and evidence based information available in the US on what was really happening in rural China. The US media had no reporting capacity on China so we were generally treated to speculation on atrocious forms of repression. From Chinese media we got only glowing propaganda about the continuing march of the glorious Revolution. Jan Myrdal's book was the first credible account of the realities of village life for average people and their families. Many reviewers regarded the book with suspicion. Americans had been indoctrinated to regard China in a totally negative way. Nothing positive about China was to be credited. I had been a student of Chinese culture since university and wrote my review in pretty much the way I characterized the book here.

A month later, a letter addressed to me arrived at the Book Center from Pantheon. The editor, Andre Schiffrin, had written to thank me for my review of *Report from a Chinese Village*. I was dumbfounded. How in the world did our little mimeographed Book Center Review end up in Andre Schiffrin office in Manhattan? Apparently, somebody in Syracuse conveyed a copy to him. In thanking me, he made what seemed like an astounding statement; he said I was one of the few reviewers who understood what Jan Myrdal was doing with this book. When Achilles was really pleased about something, he didn't become highly verbal but rather got a certain look in his eyes and his whole expression beamed in an unmistakable way. He gave me that look when he read Andre Schiffrin's letter.

The second result from writing a book review for our in-house publication emerged three years later when I was on the faculty of Friends World College. Prior to being hired by the college, I helped the president, Morris Mitchell, edit his book on world education and then shepherded it through the publication process. We had become good friends. About a year after I was hired at the college, Morris and I were having a conversation about curriculum development when he cautioned me about my views on the place of aggression in the evolution of animal behaviour and its presumed carry over to the understanding and management of human behaviour. Morris kept up on such things and it was clear he was referring to the work of Konrad Lornez as articulated in his 1965 book, *On Aggression* and to my favourable review of this book. Three years previous I had written a review of *On Aggression* for the Book Center Review in which I drew a parallel between the displacement behaviour in certain animals that forestalls aggression and the non-violent tactics of civil resistance as practiced by Gandhians, Quakers, and civil rights activists.

It was clear to me, Morris must have seen my review or had been told about it and was now concerned he had a faculty member who was apt to blur the conventionally drawn line between animal and human behaviour. Morris was a Quaker and Friends

World College was a Quaker sponsored institution committed to education for the peaceful resolution of conflict. This tradition was anchored in a high view of human spiritual development and its potential for transforming conflict and violence into problem solving and cooperation for the common good. He understood and appreciated the evolutionary worldview but was concerned that blurring the line between animal behaviour and human behaviour would denigrate the human and dilute the commitment to the peace testimony and peace work as understood and practiced by Quakers and others.

Morris wasn't the kind of person you argued with. He had been a student of John Dewey and was thoroughly imbued with the ideals of progressive education. He was a veteran of Roosevelt's New Deal ethos and now, late in life, had taken on the task of establishing a new Quaker-sponsored liberal arts college based on world education for the promotion of social change and human betterment. He was in his mid-70s. I was 31. I assured him that as a Quaker I too placed a high value on the peace testimony and had no interest in weakening it. He was suitably reassured, but I continued to wonder how he knew about my review of the Lorenz book.

He later tweaked me a bit when he introduced me to a delegation from the New York State Board of Regents as "the college's resident anarchist." He said this in a way that indicated he probably thought every college should have one, so I was not alarmed at the reference although I thought it odd because I had never brought anarchist philosophy into any of our conversations. But I did have Murray Bookchin's essay, "Ecology and Revolutionary Thought" and Paul Goodman's book, *Communitas* on a syllabus for teaching environmental studies so I suspect Morris was keeping track of my influences and interests.

•   •   •

During the years our family lived in Syracuse, we were actively associated with the Syracuse Friends Meeting. We first connected with Quakers in Iowa City and were regular attenders at the Iowa

City Friends Meeting. Ellen and I had both come from Mennonite families and had grown up in Mennonite communities so we were thoroughly imbued with the Anabaptist worldview that grew out of the Radical Reformation of 16th century Europe. A century later, the Quaker movement in England picked up this ethos of egalitarian spirituality but added to it the ethic of right relationship that encompassed a critique of the whole social and economic order. Thus began a tradition of spiritual activism with regard to the common good that has made issues of justice, cooperation, equity, peace, and human betterment frontline concerns of the Religious Society of Friends throughout its history. Our experience with the Iowa City Friends Meeting brought us fully on board with the Quaker way.

Quakerism emerged in association with the English Revolution and its aftermath in the 17th century. In the cultural upheaval of the time, Quakers broke with the dogmatic theology and clerical structure of orthodox Christendom. They proceeded to pioneer an experiential approach to spiritual life but with a compass setting derived from the ethics of the Sermon on the Mount and with openness to what they called "continuing revelation." Early Quakers distilled this process-based approach to religious understanding and spiritual life into a lived commitment to com-passion and social justice, a witness that has persisted over the centuries since.

Within these parameters, Quaker Meetings are often a mixed lot, with persons of strong and distinct convictions in attendance. This is, at least in part, why Quakers have become well practiced in mediation as well as meditation. The Syracuse Friends Meeting was no exception, although it was a little startling to find a senior member of the Meeting held political views that included support for the use of military force against the rise of Communist regimes. Such views were impossible to reconcile with the Quaker peace testimony, but in other respects Alfred Cope was a stalwart Quaker, a good member of the Meeting. His Quakerly behaviour, in another respect, left me with a book related story I have never forgotten.

Alfred Cope was Assistant Dean of the College of Liberal Arts at Syracuse University. He did something in his capacity as Assistant Dean that was pedagogically unique and warmed my book-loving heart toward him. As the story came to me, a student who was about to be expelled for reasons of behaviour and erratic academic performance ended up in Dean Cope's office. Apparently, Al Cope saw something in this young man that prompted him to offer an unusual deal. He offered to hold back on the sentence of being expelled from the university if the student would read Lewis Mumford's recently published book, *The City in History: Its Origins, Its Transformations, and Its Prospects*, and report to his office on a regular schedule to discuss the reading.

What a stroke of disciplinary and pedagogic genius! This miscreant was being offered a private tutorial on the history of civilization as a corrective for his failure to appreciate the human heritage that made it possible for there to be universities and for him to be a university student. Six hundred and fifty pages of Lewis Mumford and discussions with the Dean should do the trick. At least that must have been Alfred Cope's calculation. I never heard the details of how this deal turned out, but the story was told to me in a way that implied the corrective had worked.

• • •

In August of 1965, Ellen and I, along with our two sons, Eric and Brendan, attended the annual conference of New York Yearly Meeting of the Religious Society of Friends (Quakers) at Silver Bay on Lake George. We were there as representatives of the Syracuse Friends Meeting. In the course of the weeklong program, we attend-ed a plenary session that changed our vocational life, although this change was still connected with working in the commonwealth of books. A presentation on Friends World College (FWC) was on the program for an evening session. This caught my attention. We had heard about this project of New York Yearly Meeting while still living in Iowa City. Advance information and requests for financial support had been circulated to Quaker Meetings around the country.

Friends World College had now become a reality and was in its opening phase. The Yearly Meeting had scheduled a report from President, Morris Mitchell, and the Director of the North American Center, Arthur Meyer.

I listened with rapt attention as Morris described a curriculum of "world education" based on the study of "world problems and their emerging solutions." He sketched out the multiple and interlocking social, economic, political, and environmental crises that were negatively affecting human security and wellbeing around the world. He explained that a new kind of education was needed to understand and effectively deal with these world problems at whatever scale they manifested, whether local, national, or global. Friends World College was designed to facilitate learning without walls. It was set up to maximize experiential learning at five regional centres around the world where students, over the course of four years, would live, study, undertake research projects and do volunteer work.

Morris was charismatic and I was inspired. But what especially caught my attention was a detail of college development. The project was provisionally chartered by the New York State Board of Regents as an Institute with the expectation that its development would fulfill the requirements for the granting of a four-year liberal arts college charter. One of the requirements was the establishment of a certain size library at the North American Center. In anticipation of this requirement, the Committee on a Friends World College had sent out an appeal to Quakers across the country for the donation of books that would be appropriate for a liberal arts college library, and, in particular, books in the fields of the social sciences, international relations, economics, environmental sciences, the humanities, and worldwide cultural history. The call for book donations was hugely successful in terms of numbers and demonstrated that Quakers were indeed a book buying and book collecting community. However, the volume of donated books and the demographic they came from had created a librarian's nightmare—a situation that was revealed to me in due course and a problem to which I will return.

The information that stuck with me from Morris's presentation was the need for the College project to meet the library development requirements of the New York State Board of Regents. On our return to Syracuse, I sat down with my Olivetti and typed out a three page letter outlining a library development and book service plan for peripatetic students and sent it off to Morris Mitchell at what was known, somewhat euphemistically, as the World Headquarters of Friends World College. The College project had attracted significant support from beyond the Quaker community and had been gifted a small estate on Long Island called Harrow Hill for its base of operations. The organizing committee had chosen Long Island for its proximity to the United Nations as the area in which to locate the college. They expected its study program to have a close association with this assembly of world cultures and its international programs.

Within days I received a phone call from Arthur Meyer telling me they were interested in my library development ideas. He asked if I could come to Long Island for an interview and to speak with them about my ideas for the library. We made the trip. The conversation went well. Morris and Arthur were seriously interested in what I could bring to the development of the college, but explained that it would be two years before funds could be committed for the library work required by the New York State Board of Regents. We returned home feeling that a connection had been made and a seed planted that might well bear vocational fruit within a context of values and professional service to which we were strongly attracted.

At almost the same time, Michael Fine, the original owner of The Paper Place in Iowa City, called from Manhattan and offered me the manager's position at the Paperback Forum. Mike had been the manager for several years but was now leaving to join the Washington Square Press division of Simon and Schuster. The Paperback Forum was located at 116th and Broadway, directly across from the main entrance to the campus of Columbia University, which it served as an independent academic bookstore. I told Michael we had the prospect of joining the staff of Friends

World College in two years. He said a two-year commitment was no problem. Positions like this are changing all the time in the book business in New York City. The opportunity was appealing. We could locate on Long Island in close proximity to Friends World College, which would serve to develop our mutual interests, while I spent two years managing the Paperback Forum.

Two problems confronted me in carrying out this plan. The first was telling Achilles that I was leaving the Syracuse Book Center at the invitation of Mike Fine to take up the management of the Paperback Forum in New York. I knew of the circumstances in which Achilles and Olga's association with Michael and Marlene, and The Paper Place, came to end was tinged with disagreement and unhappiness. After the opportunities Achilles had afforded me and after all we had accomplished together, it felt a little traitorous to jump ship at Mike's invitation. But Achilles and I were close friends and had a kind of intuitive rapport that was solid and heart-felt.

I told Achilles about my communication with Friends World College and the prospect of the library development position two years hence and about Mike's call that had come at the same time. I explained that locating on Long Island while managing the store in Manhattan for two years was a way to keep in close touch with the college in anticipation of joining the staff. I needn't have worried. Achilles understood what this opportunity meant to me and was gracious in his acceptance of our decision.

The second problem was entirely my own. Did I really want to work in New York City? Good grief, no! In Syracuse, I walked to work each day in all sorts of weather and was happily ensconced in a lively and convivial bookstore environment that I had helped develop, even to the extent of building some of the fixtures. But it was the prospect of a library position with Friends World College and of being a part of its revolutionary approach to experiential world education that overcame my aversion to working temporarily in the depths of Manhattan. With the help of my mother, we bought a house in Hempstead, Long Island, a few miles from the Westbury campus of FWC, and made the move in the late summer of 1966. I became a commuter on the Long Island Railroad. It was a plunge into the maelstrom.

Chapter Three

Into the Maelstrom
The Paperback Forum, New York City

*Consider the Bookseller. You may have overlooked the
dignity of the calling: the indispensable link between the
productive brain and the eager mind.*

Charles K. Stotlemeyer
Bookseller of Hancock, Maryland

Managing an academic bookstore at 116th and Broadway in
Manhattan was, indeed, a plunge into the maelstrom. Michael
Shimkin had established The Paperback Forum in the early 60s
about a year before Michael and Marlene Fine returned to New
York City from Iowa. In offering me the manager's position, Mike
Fine filled me in on the store's history. He came into the picture at
a time when, after a year of operation, it had sustained a $10,000
pilferage loss. Mike Shimkin was the son of Leon Shimkin, the
publisher at Simon and Schuster. Mike Shimkin was also involved
in the publishing business and The Paperback Forum needed
full-time, sharp-eyed management if it was to survive. The store
had become known as an easy mark for stealing books uptown
and peddling them to used bookshops downtown. Mike Fine took
over as manager, put a stop to that, and saved the store. He was
now moving into publishing at Simon and Schuster as well.[4] This
was the legacy of management I had been tapped to continue.

---

4   Mike Fine became an acquisitions editor at Simon & Schuster's
     Washington Square Press. He was convinced there was a
     future for paperback editions of (continues on next page)

So, in addition to being literally plunged each day by the Long Island Railroad into the city, and then from Penn Station plunged by subway to 116th Street, I was now a Manhattan watchdog, alert for people entering the store in bulky coats who were clearly not students. The pilferage problem had not vanished and still required vigilance. Although cross-grained to my natural bent, I became satisfactorily adept at stopping occasional thieves at the door and removing a surprising number of books from under their coats where they had them secured between their upper arms and bodies. And then, for good measure, telling them in no uncertain terms they were not welcome in the store and would be prevented from entering should they again attempt to do so. This was mostly bluff; I couldn't be standing at the door all day watching for their return, but it let them know they were now a target for us the way our store had been a target for them. I also had several employees whose vigilance could be counted on in this regard as well. I was aware there was a certain level of danger in these confrontations but mostly the poor sods just wilted, released the books, and beat a hasty retreat back to the street. Into the maelstrom took on a variety of meanings.

As it turned out, my management stint at The Paperback Forum lasted a bit less than a year due to a new turn of events at Friends World College. Michael knew my plan was to join the staff of the College as soon as it became possible and, although disappointed that it had come sooner than expected, was pleased for me. This is what happened.

After our move to Hempstead we became closely associated with what was happening at the North American Center of the College. In particular we became well acquainted with Arthur and Jane Meyer who had three boys near the same ages as Eric and Brendan. Arthur was the director of the North American

---

hitherto unavailable modern classics in philosophy, the social sciences, and the humanities. He overcame scepticism at WSP and started by publishing mass-market editions of Sartre's *Being and Nothingness* and Freud's *Interpretation of Dreams*. He was right. They sold well and a further transformation in paperback publishing was underway.

Center. In the course of our association, he learned that Ellen was a dietician with experience in institutional food service. The couple that had been running the kitchen for the first two years of the College's operation was moving on and Arthur was searching for a replacement.

When he learned of Ellen's qualifications and experience, the tables turned on the Helmuths' timeline for joining the staff of the College. Food service outranked library development with respect to urgency and a new intake of students was due to land on campus in September. An arrangement was offered for both of us to come on staff for the fall semester of 1967. Ellen would become the food service manager. I would begin working on library development and, much to my surprise, be assigned a faculty role with regard to environmental studies. We sold our Hempstead house and moved into a campus residence in the late summer. Goodbye Long Island Railroad, goodbye subway rides, goodbye both the stress and enjoyment of managing a Manhattan bookstore at 116th and Broadway. It had been a challenge to which I rose, and I had great staff, but, truth-to-tell, The Paperback Forum had almost none of the convivial, community-based atmosphere that was the dominant characteristic of The Paper Place and Syracuse Book Center. But it had its moments and its connections, and 1967 was a pivotal year in the cultural upheaval that's part of my bookseller's memories.

• • •

In 1967, San Francisco was caught up in the Summer of Love and the wave of energy animating this cultural phenomenon was clearly evident in New York City as well. As Bob Dylan put it, " ... something's happening but you don't know what it is, do you, Mr. Jones"? For the time I was at The Paperback Forum, I had an observer's ringside seat and made the most of my Manhattan opportunity to understand what it was that was happening. Two of my student-age staff were helpful guides. Sadly, I don't remember their names but I can still see them both in my mind's eye.

The first was a graduate student working on a master's degree at Columbia. She was a bright presence at the sales counter and was one I could count on to notice unlikely customers in big coats. One summer day when she was off work, she literally came running into the store waving a book in her hand and said to me, "Keith, Keith, you've got to read this book. I've just read it and I now know what I'm going to do with my life!"

Whoa, this is big news. I'd heard a lot of good things about books in bookstores and heard fulsome praise heaped on favourite writers, but this was the first time someone had told me a book had revealed to them what they wanted to do with their life. I recognized the book; it was the Ann Arbor Paperback edition of *The Image: Knowledge in Life and Society* by Kenneth Boulding. I knew Kenneth Boulding. Kenneth Boulding was a Quaker. I had read a number of his books, but not this one. I had met him in Iowa when the American Friends Service Committee brought him to Cedar Rapids for a public lecture. He was a respected economist, a social scientist, a pioneering peace researcher, and one of the founders of an interdisciplinary field of study and research called General Systems Analysis. He later, without at first realizing it, laid down the thinking that made him a founding figure in the field of ecological economics.

The Image was a book I knew by reputation because it was known Boulding had literally dictated the text into a tape recorder and had it typed up for publication. He had that kind of mind and spoke in complete sentences. The sentences formed paragraphs and the paragraphs formed chapters virtually ready for print. He had composed *The Image* while at the Center for Advanced Studies in the Behavioral Sciences at Stanford for the academic year of 1954-55.

I obeyed my employee's command and promptly read the book. I immediately saw what made reading this book such an intellectually exciting experience and could understand why, if you had not yet encountered this kind of holistic worldview, reading it could be a life orienting experience. Boulding is a master of the kind of ecological thinking that lays out a coherent picture of the whole panorama of living phenomena, including human knowledge and complex societies. It's not often you get to see first hand the way the right book at the right time in the hands of the right person can give them a powerful impetus for what to do with their life. There's something almost sacred about such a moment, a feeling of magic in the encounter, a sense of the book as an agent of magic. Something happens that cannot be completely accounted for.

Twenty-three years later at a meeting of Friends Association for Higher Education, I told Kenneth Boulding about the day a bookstore employee came running in the door shouting, "Keith, Keith...." He said, "Really?" I replied, "Yes, really." He just beamed, and I thought what a deep satisfaction it must be to hear this about a book you had written and published over thirty years earlier.

In 1965, Kenneth gave a short talk to a group of space scientists in Seattle that has become a widely referenced and much quoted classic in the literature of ecological economics. The talk was titled, "Spaceship Earth." A year later he published an expanded essay titled "The Economics of Spaceship Earth." He was not the first to use this metaphor, but he was the first economist to fully understand its implications for the human-earth relationship. As far as I can tell from my research, Adlai Stevenson, the much-loved Governor of Illinois and Democratic candidate for President in 1952 and 1956, introduced the expression "spaceship earth" in a campaign speech. Boulding either picked up the metaphor from Stevenson or reinvented it. Following Boulding, British economist Barbara Ward used it for the title of her 1966 book, and Buckminster Fuller published a book in 1969 with the title *Operating Manual for Spaceship Earth*. It was Kenneth Boulding, however, who made the metaphor a gateway concept for understanding that the ideology of infinite growth on a finite planet was a setup for human disaster—an insight of such significance that over the ensuing years, and in the development of ecological economics, it has played a determinative role in more than one person's decision about what to do with their life, including me. *The Image,* on another level, also provides that type of insight about how the world works, the kind of insight that once you see it you cannot fail to see it ever after. Boulding was that kind of seminal thinker.

• • •

A similar experience with another employee occurred that same summer, only this time the epiphany was mine. In the course of our conversations, I must have mentioned my annoyance with the Beatles early, juvenile love songs that I heard *ad nauseam* from the outdoor loudspeaker of a record shop on Crouse Street across the corner from the Syracuse Book Center. One afternoon near the end of May in 1967, my colleague came in the store with a copy of *Sgt. Pepper's Lonely Hearts Club Band* and said, "Keith, you've got to listen to this." He handed me the album and I began to study the cover. My first reaction on gazing at the gallery of figures assembled behind the ceremonially clad Fab Four was, wait a minute, I recognize most of these people. What are they doing on the cover of a Beatles album? These are mostly famous personages from history and from both low and high culture. As a student of history and culture, my interest was piqued. If the Beatles chose to have this disparate assembly of cultural icons standing behind them on the cover of this album there must be something going on with them worth paying attention to.

Indeed, not being a Beatles fan I was unaware of the album that had preceded *Sgt. Pepper—Rubber Soul.* Nobody had called it to my attention and I wasn't otherwise paying attention to the Beatles. *Rubber Soul,* I later discovered, had signalled a seismic shift in where the Beatles were going, or, perhaps more to the point, where they had been before they cut *Rubber Soul* and now *Sgt. Pepper.* Something was happening and once I took my colleague's advice and listened to *Sgt. Pepper,* I had no doubt what it was. From another platform of observation and research, my interest in the rise of counter-culture movements in their literary, artistic, spiritual, and political expressions primed me to understand what was happening with the Beatles.

Over the last few centuries of European and American cultural life, various counter-culture movements have emerged that charted ways out from under the forms of hierarchical, self-serving, wealth accumulating oppression that various configurations of the ruling class traditionally used to maintain their domination. The struggle had been repeated so often that it has become classic in the characteristics of its societal dynamics. On the one side is the authority of a power-wielding closed mind opposing any challenge to its domination. On the other, an opening of the mind to change by the emergence of liberatory movements in religious, political, economic, artistic, literary, and social life, and the prospect of ending the domination of a ruling elite. How does the ruling class maintain its rule? The answer, in large part, is by *controlling the narratives of change.* Ever since the end of the Medieval period in Europe, when the Protestant Reformation broke with the cultural mindset of the Roman Catholic Church, and the Radical Reformation subsequently broke with the mindset of the Protestant Reformation, an on-going battle to control the narratives of change has been central to the evolution of Western Civilization, a contagion that has, in recent times, permeated most of the other cultural zones of the planet.

As Thomas Berry never tired of reminding us through his work as a cultural historian, it's all a matter of *story.* Those in power work assiduously to tell a story that's so convincing it will keep them in power. But the cultural situation, with some exceptions, is now different than it used to be when a good solid story that most everyone believed was sufficient to keep an unchanging hierarchy in power. The controlling story now has to be about change because nothing is more evident since the scientific and industrial revolutions than the trajectories of change engulfing the human project. So the ruling class, now composed of those who control and benefit most from the wealth accumulating dynamic of hyper-industrialism and the endless growth of hyper-consumption, have developed a whole industry devoted to telling the story about how, from their self-aggrandizing point of view, things are changing and what we all need to do is get on board with their story of change.

This modern storytelling, while seemingly open minded to change, is, in fact, a new orthodoxy with a mindset just as closed to any other way of life, work, and livelihood than were earlier forms of hierarchical domination and control. It is an ideology generated by the power brokers of the industrial-consumer economy and their political allies. Goethe saw it coming. Blake was alarmed at the trajectory of rapacious industrialism he saw unfolding. Wordsworth and Coleridge ran up a contrasting flag for the aesthetic imagination; a whole movement in poetry and literary culture rose up and staked out a cultural alternative to the mechanization and industrialization that was more and more colonizing the public imagination. William Morris and John Ruskin championed the ethic of craftwork, the dignity of self-directed labour, and the primacy of cooperation in civic and economic life. Robert Owen attempted to establish villages of cooperation that equitably socialized manufacturing labour and its rewards. Catholic social teachings spawned a back-to-the-land movement by a cohort of radical Catholics along with a sweeping critique of industrial capitalism, perhaps best summed up by G. K. Chesterton in his book *The Outline of Sanity*. Various other affinity groups, some religiously based and some not, pulled away from the whirlpool of the industrial-commercial way of life and established communities of self-provisioning enterprise, social cooperation, and aesthetic and spiritual contemplation.

This counter-culture movement runs like an aquifer under the history of modern Western Civilization. It periodically surfaces in spring-like expressions of renewal that challenge the trajectory of the industrial-consumer society with its war-making competition, the insecurity of its boom and bust business cycle, and its now ecologically devastating impact on earth's organic life-support systems. What we have come to know as "the 60s" was a dramatic and society rattling resurfacing of this counter-cultural tradition.

It was no coincidence that the spontaneously organized group serving up free food in San Francisco during the 1967 Summer of Love called themselves "The Diggers." One of the signal eruptions of the counter-culture movement happened in early 17th century England when Gerard Winstanley and a group of like-minded folks took over a parcel of private estate land on St. George's Hill and established both housing and self-provisioning food crop production. They became known as "the diggers" for their working of the land. The move was a deliberate and well-executed challenge to the inequity of land holding and land access for the poor.

I was a student of this history before I landed in the bookstore business at The Paper Place in Iowa City, but this employment opportunity, and then vocational choice, put me on the frontline of the counter-culture's literary and social change movements that came to indelibly mark the 60s and the decades following. At the Syracuse Book Center we picked up the alternative press newspapers as they began to appear from various cities around the country. As a result, I have an almost complete set of *The San Francisco Oracle* in the archive of my library. Starting in 1966 and running for twelve glorious issues to 1968, the *Oracle* was an exemplar of the underground press. It published Gary Snyder's hopeful and prescient essay, "Four Changes," as well as the 23,000-word transcript of a conversation between Allen Ginsberg, Timothy Leary, Alan Watts, and Gary Snyder that took place on Watt's houseboat at Sausalito. That text remains to this day a deep dive into the ethos of the counter-culture and a particularly good exploration of the role and significance of psychedelics in its eruption at this specific time. Leary, of course, comes across as the pied piper. Ginsberg is more thoughtful in his contributions than his poetry would lead you to expect. Snyder, ever the ethno-poetical anthropologist, has a world historical perspective on the use of mind-altering substances. Watts, the elder of the group, repeats the sound advice that psychedelics should be regarded as "medicine, not diet," a perception that builds on Aldous Huxley's first person report in his 1954 book, *The Doors of Perception* — a title taken from William Blake, who wrote; "If the doors of perception were cleansed everything would appear to man as it is, Infinite."

So in the summer of 1967—the Summer of Love, even in New York City—and on the strength of my employee's demand, I stopped at the record shop a block down Broadway from The Paperback Forum and purchased a copy of *Sgt. Pepper's Lonely Hearts Club Band*. That evening I put it on our small hi-fi record player and came to understand what had happened to the Beatles, what the fuss was all about, and why, as my friend, journalist Peter Stafford, later wrote, "people are now listening to the psychedelic turn in rock music the way the faithful used to listen to the reading of the scripture."

If you study the cover of the album you will find Aldous Huxley in the second row (more or less) in the upper left. They should have included William Blake and Alan Watts. Watts, in homage to Huxley, had added his report on psychedelic experience with the 1962 publication of *The Joyous Cosmology: Adventures in the Chemistry of Consciousness*. *Sgt. Pepper* was nothing if not joyous. The Beatles knew what they were doing. They were writing the next chapter in their musical idiom for the new story they felt in their bones was coming to be—a story of personal and societal transformation that would usher in an era founded on the ways of peace and good will, cooperation and sharing. This was a world many people over the course of history have longed for and worked to make real; a world many of the young at this time seemed primed for taking to heart. After all, Pete Seeger had been singing for decades "Peace on the Earth, good will to men, if there be God then that's his Word: there *shall* be peace."

The plaintive but convivial mantra in *Sgt. Pepper*, "I get by with a little help from my friends" then jumps in the next album (*Magical Mystery Tour*), to "All You Need Is Love," a song recorded with glorious orchestration, a song that begins with the French national anthem and ends with the unmistakable musical image of the Beatles as a marching band being swept up in a joyous throng trooping off down the road of the future with the repeated strains of "all you need is love" trailing ever fainter on the air.

It sounds so simplistic and perhaps a little naïve, but it is, in fact, what every great religious tradition and ethically-prompted social reform movement comes down to at the core of their insights and dreams for a better world, a peaceful and compassionate human world and a human world in harmony with the great, all encompassing natural world on which human welfare depends. With *Sgt. Pepper*, the Beatles exploded popular music. With a salute to psychedelic experience that outclassed the preaching of Tim Leary, the Beatles jumped to the head of the counter-culture movement with both the *joie de vivre* of "Lucy in the Sky with Diamonds" and the soulful warning of "She's Leaving Home." Something, indeed, was happening, and, with the release of *Sgt. Pepper*, the Beatles had run up an infectious musical flag that unfurled a new riff on the story.

• • •

During my time working in Manhattan, I took advantage of the opportunity to connect with people and places that figured significantly in my ongoing research and in my vocation as bookseller. Getting to know Peter Stafford and collaborating with him was a particularly rewarding connection. Peter and Bonnie Golightly had co-authored the book *LSD: The Problem Solving Psychedelic*, which was published in January of 1967. As a journalist, he had contributed articles on the history and contemporary trajectory of various psychedelic substances into medical research and popular culture. Peter was one of the few people, along with Alan Watts who were offering seriously considered, well balanced, thoughtful, and helpful guidance on the use, management, and potentially positive effects of the various psychedelics that were coming into prominence.

It was clear the effect on consciousness of these various chemical compounds was a disturbingly powerful experience. Huxley's second essay on this subject, *Heaven and Hell*, (a title also taken from William Blake — *The Marriage of Heaven and Hell*) published in 1956 and later combined with *Doors of Perception*, signalled the extremes that could be triggered by psychedelics. Huxley, Watts, Snyder, Stafford, and a few other figures of note offered the beginnings of guidance for the intelligent management of this new, yet old, factor in cultural life. Helpful advice was also coming from the medical field of psychiatric research but it was much limited in circulation.

Tim Leary, bless his heart, which was in the right place, took up the challenge of educating the broader public about the potential of psychedelic experience to usher in a transcendent level of consciousness and thus, as he saw it, transform societal relations toward the compassionate, cooperative, spiritually minded world of which mystics and sages had long dreamed. Unfortunately, he misjudged the receptivity of mainstream society to his message. After alarming the guardians of convention and prompting the enactment of legal sanctions, Leary veered into the role of a guru trying to galvanize a new religion. He was right in thinking that the power of the substances he was dealing with had the potential to catalyze profound spiritual experience — he and his colleagues at Harvard had proved that with their Good Friday experiment in the College Chapel — but then aiming to initiate a new counter-culture religion was a target that took him beyond the role of societal reformer and into the wilds of an underground existence that dissipated his charisma.

Meanwhile, people like Peter Stafford carried on in a balanced and helpful way with regard to understanding, appreciating, and, so-to-speak, domesticating the potential of psychedelics within the realms of ordinary personal and professional life; thus the title and orientation of his book — *LSD: The Problem Solving Psychedelic.*

I first met Peter when I attended a presentation he made based on his book. I was struck by the levelheaded, objective tone he struck in discussing a subject that tempted others into superlatives. In addition, he had an interest in the potential for psychedelic experience as it became increasingly wide-spread for effecting positive changes throughout society. For example, being touched by an overwhelming sense of compassion, which is one of the common experiences, might well lead to a reduction of intolerance at the social level and the crafting of more generous and equitable public policies at the political level. This was a potential that caught my interest as well. After several conversations we teamed up on a presentation we called "Psychedelics and Social Change" that we gave at the Psychedelic Information Center in mid-town Manhattan.

We were also both interested in the potential of the carefully moderated use of psychedelics for enhanced learning and for what Peter called "problem solving." Through my association with Friends World College, and in anticipation of joining the staff in the not to distant future, I was already thinking about the way its curriculum was being developed. And I knew for sure that students coming into the program were bound to be above average in their familiarity with the range of exotic substances in circulation. Students yet to be exposed were bound to get exposed within the context of the College program. Think about it; after a semester orientation at the campus on Long Island, students would be off to Mexico and then Europe, East Africa, India, and Japan in the course of the four year program. It seemed to me somebody ought to be thinking long and hard about the kind of guidance that could help reduce the risk of harm and provide an orientation of management for potential benefit.

I knew this would be a hard sell with the college administration and perhaps with students as well, but for opposite reasons. College administrators want to discourage such experimentation and then look the other way when students are not deterred. Students, being inducted by their peers into experiences the adults around them don't want them to have, are not likely to listen up when precautionary guidance is offered, at least not until the lack of sound management results in a crisis either for themselves or one of their friends. Nonetheless, Peter Stafford and I were thinking about such things and wondering how such guidance might be effectively approached. We were both old enough that we were "looking through the other end of the telescope," so-to-speak, wondering about what was to come and how best to be helpful.

Through the chaos of unsuccessful legal repression, personal and social harm, lack of guidance for positive outcomes, the pro-liferation of underground manufacture and the contamination of the substances that was yet to come — through all this, and more, Peter's book remains a beacon of common sense and good judgment in a field of research that was just opening. Perhaps we should have known that the dam was breaking and that the chances of a socially responsible and flow of these extraordinary substances into primarily beneficial uses was marginal at best and likely remote.

Peter would be heartened that, in recent years, after the long proscription of psychedelics, research is again being conducted and guided use is being provided that bodes well for their beneficial effects both personally and for society as whole. Peter Stafford, the cheerful, kindly, good-natured person that he was, never lost faith in his project and continued to chronicle and document this aspect of the culture of social change over the next 40 years.

•   •   •

In addition, I used my Manhattan time to conduct forays into the book culture of the city. In particular, I made regular stops at Ted and Elias Wilentz's 8th Street Bookshop in Greenwich Village, which was the east coast counterpart to Lawrence Ferlinghetti's City Lights Bookstore in San Francisco, both being oases of literary culture. The Paperback Forum was an academic bookstore specializing in a comprehensive inventory of paperback books oriented toward the graduate students and faculty at Columbia University. Walking into the 8th Street Bookshop was to be immersed in the top level of serious literature being published as well as a deep inventory of the avant-garde writing and small press publications.

My Manhattan bookstore pilgrimages regularly included Ed Sanders' Peace Eye Bookstore way over in what was then called the East Village. Ed Sanders was a militant poet who went to jail for protesting against nuclear armed submarines. His shop stocked the best and latest books on radical politics and the peace movement. It had a great poetry section with books you couldn't find anywhere else, along with the farthest out counter-culture literature being published.

The third bookshop on my itinerary was the Paragon Book Gallery at 140 East 59th Street, which billed itself as "The Oriental Bookstore of America." The first time I walked into this unique emporium, I had a small version of the feeling that came over me when I walked into the exhibit titled *Chinese Art Treasures* when it was on display at the Museum of Contemporary Art in Chicago in 1961. This traveling selection of work from the Palace Museum Collection presented the epitome of Chinese art spanning eight thousand years. It had been curated from the part of the Collection that had been packed up and hidden in the early 1930s to secure it from falling into the hands of the Japanese army that was advancing toward Beijing. The best of the hidden collection was taken to Taiwan in 1948 and 1949 by the Chaing Kai-shek government as it prepared to flee the mainland in advance of the Red Army's victory in the Chinese civil war. The 1961 American tour of the Chinese Art Treasures exhibit was the first time any of the Palace Museum Collection had been seen outside China.

We were living in Iowa City at the time and twice made the trip to Chicago, once when the exhibit opened and again just before it closed. The experience of viewing and standing in the presence of such a powerful yet subtle representation of Chinese art and culture was a once in a lifetime event. The exhibit catalogue, a nearly three hundred page, 9 x 11 inch book, remains one of the most treasured volumes in my library. It was produced by Editions de'Art Albert Skira of Geneva and includes tipped in color plates of exquisite quality. I was at the time studying with Professor Y. P. Mei who had recently established the Chinese and East Asian Studies program at the University of Iowa. To have the Palace Museum Collection on its American tour at the very time I was immersed in the study of Chinese art and culture was an extraordinary stroke of serendipity, which I incorporated in my response to the course and seminar work of the program.

Although I was still an undergraduate, Professor Mei allowed me to take all the English-based courses in the program with the understanding I would not expect a degree in this specialty because, apparently, he knew I would not likely master the language-learning component. How he knew, I was not quite sure, but I agreed. This gentle Confucian scholar was an astute judge of character and intention. We had become friends. He liked my essays on Chinese landscape painting and on Taoism and Buddhism, but he could tell I didn't have what it takes to learn Mandarin. He was certainly correct in this assessment.[5]

The Chinese Art Treasures exhibit was arranged so the first thing you saw, singularly framed by the entrance doorway, was a painting of a contemplative figure sitting under a gnarled tree with a small scroll laid out beside his folded leg. His gaze, however, is slightly lifted into the near distance as if pondering what he has been reading. As I walked through the entrance, this exquisite rendering of a quintessential figure of Chinese culture stopped me in my tracks. The effect was so moving I had to wipe tears from my eyes to keep the painting in focus. In that moment, I was seeing and feeling a universal ideal of all cultures that have developed a contemplative dimension. And, perhaps subtly intending to make the point that the exhibit was presenting the collective achievement of a culture, the painting that welcomed the visitor, and is on the cover of the exhibit catalogue, is by an artist whose name is unknown. The display sign read simply: "Anonymous: Noble Scholar under a Willow. Eleventh century, Sung dynasty." This signalled the communal feeling across the reach of centuries that was the ethos of this exhibit.

This is such a contrast with the individualistic focus and cultural ethos of European and American art. Something very different was going on here and I was primed to "get it." The era of the 60s was underway and it came for me with a spiritual boost from the Palace Museum Collection.

---

5   I barely passed my German course requirement at university, which was ironic because my ancestral background is German-Swiss and my father spoke the variety of German known as Pennsylvania Dutch. The graduate student who taught my German course, under the supervision of Professor Fred Fehling, was indulgent when he recognized my difficulty and gave me a passing grade I probably didn't deserve.

Discovering the Paragon Book Gallery five years later was a delightful replay of the ambiance in which I had been immersed during my studies with Professor Mei. I am blessed with the ability to walk into a bookstore or a library and get carried away by what I discover. A hitch in time seems to occur from which I sometimes have to be extracted by Ellen if she has accompanied me, although she can get similarly waylaid by a good cookbook section. It was not only the books on Chinese landscape painting—a genre by which I am incurably mesmerized—but the excellent selection of East Asian books on what Western scholarship calls philosophy and religion that made me a regular visitor to the Paragon Book Gallery.

In particular, I was elated to find on the shelf before me R. H. Blyth's legendary four-volume set, compiled by seasons, of the history of Japanese haiku. These books are essentially comprehensive anthologies with Blyth's running commentary, which in itself is a masterpiece of idiosyncratic scholarship. I had previously read his extraordinary book, *Zen in English Literature and Oriental Classics*, and had seen tantalizing references to the haiku books, not least of which was Jack Kerouac's comment about seeing them on the shelf at Gary Snyder's neatly kept and sparsely appointed cabin on Mount Tamalpias above Mill Valley in California. As a bookstore manager and buyer, I could have searched out a source for the set but had not done so. Now, here they were, at hand, waiting for me, so-to-speak.

But beyond even this discovery at the Paragon Book Gallery, I found a multi-volume set of Blyth's books of which I was unaware. Reginald Horace Blyth was an English scholar who, after teaching in Korea from 1925 to 1935, settled in Japan where he spent the rest of his life. He was interred as an enemy alien during World War Two. He later taught at Gakushuin University and became the private tutor to the Crown Prince Akihito. He was a friend of D. T. Suzuki, the scholar whose work first introduced Zen Buddhist studies to Europe and the Americas.

Some time before 1960, Blyth laid out an eight-volume project titled, *Zen and Zen Classics*. And now, to my great delight, here on the shelf at Paragon were five of the volumes, all but one published by The Hokuseido Press in 5 x 7 inch hardback bindings — altogether lovely, small books. Volume 1, subtitled *From the Upanishads to Huineng*, had been published in 1960. A flyer that came with the book indicates what a treat the reader is in for. It starts like this:

> In this, the first of eight volumes, Zen is treated with a certain nonchalance, not to say rudeness, and this should give the reader confidence that he is not being swindled or mystified into accepting some kind of wooly theosophy...

> One characteristic of this book should not be overlooked, the element of humour, without which Zen itself can hardly exist. The quips and quotations at the head of each page are themselves worth whatever the price of the book is. Indeed, it may be safely affirmed that this small volume is indispensable to anyone who doesn't particularly want to know what Zen is.

After reading this and savouring the feel and look of each volume with their illustrations and rice paper fly-leafs, I stacked them up and headed for the sales counter.

As it turned out, the five volumes I secured with my purchase are almost all that ever came to be published of this project. Some of the volumes seem to have been composed from material Blyth had previously written and some written specifically for the project. Volume 2, *History of Zen, 713-867*, was published in 1964, the year the author died. Volume 4, *Mumonkan*, was published in 1966. Volume 7, *Twenty-five Essays*, was published earlier, in 1962. Volume 8, *Buddhist Sermons on Christian Texts*, had been published still earlier in a 1952 paperback edition by Kokudosha. Since Blyth listed this earliest book as the final volume of the set, he must have seen it as a fitting conclusion to the project, which indeed it is. The title alone is enough to make you sit up straight and take notice. This 93-page book is composed of single paragraph "sermons" and occasionally just aphoristic notes on biblical texts, along with comparable quotations from Buddhist literature. This cross-cultural juxtaposition is done in such a generous and disarming way it makes you want to read the Christian and Jewish scriptures again with new eyes. R. H. Blyth put a unique touch of serious ebullience and an appreciation of trickster-like conundrums into everything he wrote.

According to the publisher's original listing of titles for this project, the volumes missing from my set are # 3, History of Zen, 867-1260, # 4, History of Korean Zen, and # 6, History of Japanese Zen. The current Wikipedia bibliography shows that volume 3 was published in 1970. But it fails to show volume 8, *Buddhist Sermons on Christian Texts* as part of the project. Since this book was included on the original list, presumably prepared by the author who was still alive at the time, its disappearance may be due to a later editorial decision at Hokuseido—I would say an editorial mistake. *Buddhist Sermons on Christian Texts* is probably the best book of the lot for the way it casts an ethos of cross-cultural and universal sympathy over the human predicament and acknowledges without closure the quest for clarity and grounding that the human spirit nonetheless holds in view and, on occasion, achieves. A nice hint of this grace can be seen in a poem R. H. Blyth wrote as he prepared for death.

Sazanka ni kokoro nokoshite tabidachinu

I leave my heart
    to the sasanqua flower
        on the day of this journey

•   •   •

It was with an ironic and mild dread that I committed to becoming a commuter on the Long Island Railway. It would have made more sense to have taken an apartment on the upper west side of Manhattan near The Paperback Forum and continued with the convenience of walking to work that I enjoyed in Syracuse. My position at the Forum had come with a generous salary so we could probably have afforded an apartment suitable for a family of four. We could have enjoyed Riverside Park along the Hudson with sons, Eric and Brendan — now robust toddlers — as we had enjoyed Thornden Park near our house in Syracuse. The great green gem of Central Park would have been only a short subway or bus ride away. We could have made pilgrimages to Central Park's small lake where E. B. White's character, Stuart Little, had his famous sailing adventure. We could have haunted the Museum of Natural History to our heart's content and availed ourselves of the resources of the New York Public Library. But my position at The Paperback Forum had a two-year timeline with the expectation of joining the staff of Friends World College as the librarian so we located in Hempstead, Long Island near the Westbury campus and I became a commuter.

It was with a sense of life-style compromise that I took on the role of long distance commuter — something I never imagined I would do. Then, to somewhat plagiarize the title of a famous Broadway play, movie, and book, "an interesting thing happened on the way to the Forum," I discovered I had two uninterrupted hours each day for reading. The morning ride from the Hempstead station to the City and back again in the evening took the better part of an hour each way and I had no problem, for the duration, of settling into whatever book I was reading at the time. What a gift! That period of time is especially vivid in memory because my reading was concentrated on the works of Herbert Read and Lewis Mumford, two major figures in my ongoing research and study.

Herbert Read had come to my attention while still in Iowa City. I previously mentioned my regular browsing in the used bookroom at Iowa Book and Supply but I forgot to mention one of the significant finds I made there — an undated, hardback, Pantheon edition of Herbert Read's *Education Through Art*. (On checking the bibliography of Read's work, it appears this book was first published by Faber and Faber in the U.K. in 1925 and then in the US in 1954, which I take to be the Pantheon edition.) One look at the table of contents and I could see there was a whole education here in one book on a subject that intrigued me. But it was the epigraph the author had put on the title page that made me carry it to the sales desk. It was a quote from Bernard Shaw: "I am simply calling attention to the fact that fine art is the only teacher except torture."

A book with an epigraph like this signals a good deal about the author's worldview and it made me want to explore this book further. I knew nothing about Herbert Read at the time. (George Bernard Shaw, I knew—how could you avoid him? I could well imagine him snorting with satisfaction after having coined this aphorism.) When I read *Education Through Art*, it put to rest for me the debate about whether the experience of beauty was simply an arbitrary and subjective event in the eye of the beholder or if it was intrinsic to the structural and functional relationships that exist between organisms and between organisms and their environments. Read was not only in the first rank as a scholar of the culture of art, he was also well versed in biology and the sciences of perception and psychology. His book made clear to me that the debate about beauty was settled on the side of the latter understanding. The processes of perception that result in the experience of "beauty" are not icing on the cake of human development and achievement, they are intrinsic to the composition of the whole cake and to the relationships of structure and function of the organic world of which humans are a part. It has to do with the unity of form expressing both diversity and harmony across the whole spectrum of the living world and the geo-chemical-physical environment in which the relationships and processes of life continue to unfold.[6]

Having read *Education Through Art*, I went in search of other books by Herbert Read and soon realized that although his forte was in the history and cultural analysis of art, he was a

---

6   For a further exploration of this study see David Rothenberg's 2011 book, *Survival of the Beautiful: Art, Science, and Evolution.*

classic "man of letters" with expertise in literature and language, social philosophy, the science of perception, Jungian psychology, environmental issues, and matters of societal structure and development. In addition, he was a fine poet, a playwright, a novelist, and a biographer. Politically, he considered himself an anarchist, which was interesting for a person so well placed in the upper level of British intelligentsia. He had an insightful perspective on almost everything happening on the contemporary cultural scene.

I began to selectively collect his already published books and keep an eye out for new ones. I was intrigued by his writings on anarchism; they were lively and instructive, but mostly derivative. I had already read much of the primary literature in this field of political and social philosophy. It was his writing on the nature of art and its social significance that was most interesting to me since it was an area of intellectual and cultural history I had not yet systematically explored. Herbert Read proved to be an exceptionally companionable instructor. I used my daily "time out" as a commuter on the Long Island Railroad to read *Icon and Idea: The Function of Art in the Development of Human Consciousness, Art and Society, The Origin of Form in Art,* and *The Form of Things Unknown: An Essay on the Impact of the Technological Revolution on the Creative Arts.*

At the same time, I was also systematically immersed in the works of Lewis Mumford, who was in many ways an American counterpart to Herbert Read, both men being polymath scholars and holistic thinkers. My second encounter with Mumford — his essay, *The Human Way Out,* being the first — was again in those seminal and halcyon Iowa City days when Gerald Stevenson put me onto a 1200-page 1956 book titled, *Man's Role in Changing the Face of the Earth.* This book was composed of the papers and discussion summaries of a 1955 international symposium convened under this same title and held at Princeton University. The event — three years in the planning — was sponsored by the Werner-Gren Foundation for Anthropological Research and organized by Carl Sauer, Marston Bates, and Lewis Mumford.

I was especially taken by Mumford's closing address to the symposium. This event, and this book, heralded a convergence of attention and growing alarm over the trajectory of human modification of the surface of the earth and the ecological effect on its biological and geophysical processes. Although individual researchers, and natural history scholars — not to mention poets and artists — had for some time been warning against the outcome of accelerating environmental degradation, this symposium was the first comprehensive assessment and report on where human adaptation to earth's environment had come from, what it was currently doing to the integrity of earth's ecosystems, and what the likely outcome would be if current forms of exploitation and maladaptation continued unabated. Sad to say, sixty years later, with a climate catastrophe closing in and earth's biodiversity plunging precipitously, we can't claim we weren't warned.

With his ecological orientation, holistic thinking, and "big history" approach, Lewis Mumford was subsequently unrelenting in his research and writing on behalf of understanding human adaptation and the increasingly desperate need for a course correction. In a late life interview he said he would die a happy man if he knew it could be written on his gravestone that none of the dire things he had forecast had come to pass.

By 1961, I had read several of Mumford's early books: *The Story of Utopias* (1922), *The Golden Day: A Study in American Literature and Culture* (1926), *Art and Technics* (1952), and *The Transformations of Man* (1956). Then came *The City in History* (1961) on which I have already commented. A book does not often daunt me, but this one was an exception. It was not so much the length but the feeling I had some catching up to do with Mumford books I had not yet read as a way of preparing for the plunge into this one. Meanwhile, in 1964, The Conservation Foundation convened another major conference that brought together over forty scholars from many relevant disciplines to consider the "future environments of North America." Again, Lewis Mumford was involved and was invited to offer closing remarks. F. Fraser Darling and John P. Milton edited the conference proceedings into a nearly 800-page book published in 1965 with the title, *Future Environments of North America: Transformations of a Continent.* Contributors to the conference and the book included Kenneth Boulding, Lynton K. Caldwell, and Ian L. McHarg. The conference contributions of many other significant scholars concerned with the effects of human adaptation to earth's ecosystems and geographic zones are included in the book as well, but the three noted above have been of particular significance for me. Kenneth Boulding has already appeared in this narrative. Lynton Caldwell and Ian McHarg will appear in due course.

Meanwhile, between Lewis Mumford's summary contribution to the 1955 symposium, *Man's Role in Changing the Face of the Earth,* and his closing presentation to the 1964 conference, *Future Environments of North America,* the trajectory of environmental degradation had grown more ominous and the mood darker. Mumford's look into the future was couched in even more dire terms. As he began, he told the assembly that rather than summarize the thrust of the conference, which is expected of the closing speaker, he wanted to talk about themes of significance and items of importance the conference had not dealt with but which were critical for understanding the scale and effect of the social-environmental-economic crisis in which technologically dominated, industrial-consumer societies were now enmeshed. Mumford, at that time, was nearly 70, with much of his major work accomplished.[7] He had no reason to soft pedal his analysis of what was likely to happen to the future environments of North America if the current socio-economic trends and conditions continued on their present course. With the juxtaposition of these two major environmental assessments a decade apart, and Lewis Mumford figuring significantly in both of them, I set my research sights on reading the work that gave him the role he now played in this cross-disciplinary attention to the realities of social ecology and human adaptation.

---

7   Mumford's last major work is a two-volume study titled *The Myth of the Machine.* Volume one is subtitled *Technics and Human Development* (1967). Volume two is subtitled *The Pentagon of Power* (1970).

I began with *Technics and Civilization* (1934), *The Culture of Cities* (1938), *The Condition of Man* (1944), and *The Conduct of Life* (1951). Along with Herbert Read's aforementioned volumes, these Mumford titles were my railway ride companions. This reading of Mumford was especially timely. It put me in a good place for my next step as a worker in the commonwealth of books. I was about to become involved in editing a book on the very kind of education Mumford was actively advocating.

•   •   •

In the year before joining the staff of Friends World College, I was drawn into helping the college president, Morris Mitchell, prepare the manuscript of his book on world education for publication. Morris was keen to get his book published in order to have it as a tool for promoting the College in general and for fund-raising in particular. Not only was he in the position of assuring the New York State Board of Regents that Friends World was on the way to meeting the requirements for a college charter, he was also aiming for eventual accreditation by the Middle States Commission on Higher Education (MSCHE). At the same time, Morris had a backup plan. Should accreditation by the MSCHE not be forthcoming, he was thinking about taking the lead in forming a new association of educational institutions that, like Friends World, were experientially based, globally oriented, and pedagogically progressive. He had a list of potential candidates. He saw the publication of his book, *World Education: Revolutionary Concept*, as an important asset for the pursuit of these goals.

When I came on the scene, the manuscript was essentially complete except for the usual front and back matter. That was not difficult to attend to but parts of the manuscript were definitely not ready for publication. Morris wanted to move on this as rapidly as possible and the manner in which he was set to do so threw up a big red flag for me. Morris had already contracted with Vantage Press to publish his book and I knew Vantage Press. They would go to print with whatever the author provided. This was a self-publishing deal with what in those days was called a vanity press. Morris was paying them to print and "publish" his book. Vantage Press had no editorial skin in the game. They would simply create the print-ready layout from Morris's manuscript, run off the number of copies he was paying for and happily see the whole print run out the door and into the author's hands. Although the Vantage Press name would be on the book, they did not function as a real publisher. They cared not at all about the quality of the books they printed or what happened to them. When I got involved, I could see an embarrassment coming if Morris's manuscript went to print as it now stood.

Although not yet an experienced editor, I had done a lot of reading of good writers and worked with editors on a variety of published essays. I had written numerous book reviews and put together a variety of newsletters. In addition, I had gleaned several themes and relevant quotations on the future of higher education from Lewis Mumford's writing that fit Morris's vision like a silk glove. I offered to integrate this supporting material and in general revise the first part of the book, which dealt with the conceptual aspects of world education. (The second part of the book was mostly reports on curriculum development and on the first two years of FWC's operation.) Morris appreciated the offer. When I showed him a sample of what I had in mind by way of revision, he gave me *carte blanche* with gratitude. We worked together from then on until I was roughly satisfied with the result and Morris was more than satisfied.

As mentioned earlier, Morris was not a person you argued with. He was used to holding court, so-to-speak. He had come to Friends World after retiring from his position as founder and Director of The Putney Graduate School of Teacher Education. He had the easy going but commanding persona of a classic southern gentleman. But as we worked on the book, he had no resistance to the revisions I introduced into his manuscript. Apparently, I understood his philosophy and worldview so well that when he saw I was improving its presentation, he would say, "That's right. That's exactly what we are talking about."

And so my first effort at editing work passed into print. Morris proved to be a good bookseller, although he also presented complimentary copies of the book to a lot of key people, some in gratitude for past support and some in anticipation of support yet to come. I see things in the book now that make me cringe a bit, but this association with Morris Mitchell overrides that reaction and the memory of our mutual dedication to articulating a new kind of higher education comes back to me with the strength of a real possession. Forms of education that foster a multi-cultural worldview along with a commitment to social justice, human betterment, and a mutually enhancing human-earth relationship are needed now more than ever.

• • •

My plunge into the Manhattan maelstrom of bookstore management was thus shorter than anticipated but I did depart The Paperback Forum with a major accomplishment for the store under my belt. Unlike The Paper Place and the Syracuse Book Center, which were both in the process of acquiring inventory when I took on the management role, the Forum had been well stocked for several years before I came on the scene; in fact, it was overstocked. In section after section, the shelves were tightly packed making it hard to find room for the new books I was bringing in. It was clear many books had been on the shelves a long time, perhaps from when the store opened in the early 60s and were more-or-less dead stock. This is always a judgment call, especially in an academic bookstore. You never know when a faculty member on a research project or a student, who has been given a must-read title by a professor, will come in the store looking for a title that by now has a covering of dust on the top edge of its text block.

Nonetheless, there comes the time in good management practice when the culling must start, dead stock pulled from the shelves, and put on sale. This is not a negative move; in fact, it generates a flurry of excited browsing by regular patrons. Prominent street-facing sale signage brings in new customers. The two-sided island shelf units on the floor of the Forum were about average eye-level in height with wide covered tops. This surface made an ideal place for the culled books to be displayed adjacent to their subject areas. If you wanted to see which titles from the Russian history section were on sale, you knew exactly where to go. I marked them at 40% off and lined them up spine-out in long rows.

The speed with which those lines of books were picked, rung through the check-out counter, and disappeared out the door was indeed satisfying. Not only did we gain the space needed for incoming books, we generated a cash flow from books that had not paid their rent. At 40% off the retail price, the store more-or-less broke even. After the major sell-off subsided, I continued with an ongoing sale section. I had by no means culled all the stock eligible, so at a reduced rate of flow we were able to keep up this incentive to stop by the Forum for a browse. Book lovers love to browse and a continually renewed sale section caters to this pleasure.

I then tackled a second and more problematic dead stock situation. The backstock shelves in the basement were loaded with multiple copies of books that had previously been ordered for course use at Columbia but had not been returned to the publisher at the conclusion of whatever semester they were for. Returning overstock to publishers is a regular procedure in the retail book business. Publishers normally set a timeline within which books can be returned and require return permission. I could tell by surveying the surplus course books that many of them were likely long past their return date. Researching the invoice file proved my hunch correct. I first dispatched the titles that were still within the permission timeline. Barely a dent had been made. The bulk of the titles were ineligible for return. I decided to play another card. I composed a letter explaining I was a new manager at The Paperback Forum and was in the process of dealing with a backlog of inventory control matters and could your office assist me in this task by granting return permission for the following titles and quantities even though the designated deadline for their return had passed.

As it turned out, I was pleased and somewhat astounded by the response. In no case was my request turned down. In a few cases, I received a telephone call from a person responsible for granting returns permission who wanted further clarification around my request. Each case ended with permission granted. I had a feeling of real accomplishment when the last of those books were out the door and substantial credit notes were received that reduced the store's outstanding balance with the publishers involved. To have implemented this workaround for gaining exemptions to publishers' return deadlines was a bit of a coup. The only wrinkle in the operation came when I moved a cluster of boxes packed for shipment to the sidewalk just outside the front door for the convenience of the freight truck driver making the pickup. Within minutes we were ticketed by an over zealous NYPD officer who said there was a city ordinance against blocking the sidewalk and here is your summons to appear in court to pay the fine.

What? The boxes are stacked against the building wall! Nobody walks there. We're not blocking the sidewalk. Sorry, bud, that's the ordinance. No blocking the sidewalk. So I had my little day in police court, paid the fine, and hoped this would be my only bookseller's brush with the law during my sojourn at 116th and Broadway in "the city that never sleeps" and has cops on the beat that give booksellers no quarter.

When the day came for my last commuter ride home on the Long Island Railway, it was with the knowledge that my vocation in the commonwealth of books was taking a turn into library development for a college on the frontlines of experiential education aimed at social change for human betterment; a circumstance in which vocation and values would now be fully aligned.

Chapter Four

From Bookseller to Librarian
Friends World College,
Long Island, and East Africa

It is likely that libraries will carry on and survive, as long as we persist in lending words to the world that surrounds us, and storing them for future readers. So much has been named, so much will continue to be named that ... we will not give up this small miracle that allows us a ghost of an understanding.

Alberto Manguel
The Library at Night

When Morris Mitchell first accompanied me to the seminar building on the North American campus of Friends World College (FWC) and explained the way he wanted the new library arranged, we again recognized an affinity of purpose in our association. He told me he wanted the first placement of shelves and books to be on the walls of the large seminar room. He said having the core library in this space would give students and faculty a sense of the surrounding presence of the great thinkers, the research scholars, and the courageous activists who had created the moral legacy of human betterment to which the curriculum of the College was devoted. He didn't have to explain to me why this arrangement was important and how it worked. The bookstores of my past had schooled me well in this experience. We were definitely on the same page about the physical design of the library and its ambient influence on the ethos of the college and its pedagogic process.[8]

A small start on the library had been made with a selection from the books that had been donated to the college. A large number of boxes crammed with donated books yet to be sorted were stored in the basement of the college headquarters at Harrow Hill. Investigating the value of these books for the college library was on my agenda. But first, in the interest of securing a liberal arts college charter from the New York State Board of Regents as soon as possible, I was provided with a $10,000 budget for the purchase of new books that were highly relevant to the scope of the college's curriculum. I assembled a file of publisher's catalogues and proceeded to order relevant titles from their backlists.

Thanks to my years managing bookstores in academic settings, I knew which publishers had the books we needed to build up a core library for FWC. I scanned new releases as new catalogues came in. In addition, I established an account with a wholesale book distribution warehouse — the name of which escapes me — on midtown Manhattan's west side. I regularly assembled a list of books I wanted to add to the library, checked the distributor's inventory against my list, placed the order, and drove to the city for pick up. While there they let me browse the warehouse shelves where I found other books I was not aware of that fit the acquisition profile for the FWC library. The core curriculum of the college included global history, cross-cultural studies, social justice, international relations, peace studies, community economic development, social ecology, and environmental studies.

•　　•　　•

---

8   I have published a more detailed account of FWC that appears under the title "The Evolution of Environmental Education: The Early Years of Friends World College, 1965 to 1970." It appears as a chapter in my 2015 book, *Tracking Down Ecological Guidance* and online at https://sckool.org/the-early-years-of-friends-world-college.html

Morris Mitchell characterized the college curriculum as focused on "world problems and their emerging solutions." By world problems he meant the kind of economic, social, political, cultural, and environmental problems that were creating crisis situations for human relations and environmental adaptation worldwide. By emerging solutions he meant the kind of cooperative, justice-based, resource-sharing, peace-building, habitat-conserving and environment-enhancing policies and programs that universally address the genuinely progressive goals of human betterment.

At our current stage of the human enterprise, many problems of human relations and environmental adaptation that flare up locally and regionally are, indeed, world problems: the global spread of resource domination by trans-national corporations, exploitational wealth-seeking, cultural and ethnic marginalization, suicidal war-making technologies, and environmental degradation among them. Addressing this range of crisis situations at local, regional, and global levels requires a new kind of education, the kind of education that Friends World College had set out to model and develop. This included establishing study centres in each of the world's major cultural regions and taking its curriculum from these real world settings and their distinctive engagements with "world problems and their emerging solutions."

Scholars interested in educational innovation observed that the FWC program would challenge graduate students and wondered if undergraduates could cope with such an intellectually and emotionally immersive course of study and research. The caution was well put, and the results of student participation in the program as it developed were uneven, sometimes dramatically so. But the effect of the opportunities created by the FWC program was also to attract students with a certain cast of mind and exploratory spirit, students who were keen for learning through real-world experience rather than through classroom-constrained and teacher-dominated processing.

This was the mid-60s. College students were rebelling across the country at the irrelevance of the traditional curriculum. University students and some faculty were in an uproar about their institution's ties to the military-industrial complex. Extra-curricular teach-ins were being organized that presented radical critiques of both university governance and the outrageous violence that the American government was visiting on the people of Vietnam. Sit-ins were happening in administration buildings and universities were being temporarily shut down in response. What a time to start a new college! But it was the right time to establish a college with a program like Friends World. In a sense, the orientation and challenge of the program selected the students that enrolled. A notable affinity emerged among the students of those early years that to this day, over fifty years later, has remained alive in a network of communication and association. Recent Friends World College reunions have been extraordinarily soulful, reconnecting experiences.

Although Morris Mitchell's concept of experiential world education set the stage for FWC's program of study and research, it was the particular cast of students attracted to the opportunity that made the project a success. Friends World College, as a small, independent institution of higher education with learning centres around the planet operated until 1991 when it became a program of Long Island University. The financial realities of maintaining the college as an independent institution had become increasingly difficult. The opportunity to pass the program on to Long Island University kept the vision of its founders alive and the experiential pedagogy of Morris Mitchell operational.

LIU carried the project forward as the Friends World Program of Long Island University. The name was eventually changed to Global College of LIU and recently to LIU Global. LIU has continued to reference the Quaker origins of its Global program. The design of the program has remained essentially as it was established when FWC was founded. The students of LIU Global have similar opportunities and comparable real world learning experiences. At the 50th Anniversary Celebration, hosted by LIU, students currently in the program talked enthusiastically about their experiences in much the same way students in the early years of FWC described the impact of what they were learning.

The tradition of experience-based, cross-cultural, world education was being carried on in the way those of us present at the founding hoped would find traction and endure.

A conversation with a senior student has stayed with me as emblematic of world education. In 1969 he had returned to the North American Center after three years of living and studying in Mexico, Europe, East Africa, India, and Japan. He had returned to FWC's Long Island campus to complete his senior thesis and had asked me to be his faculty advisor for this last period of his work with the college.

In the course of our discussions about how his thesis was shaping up, he stopped at one point and said, "You know, Keith, I no longer think like an American." Clearly, his globally based, cross-cultural education had effected this transformation in worldview. World education had created a world citizen. What more could we hope for in pioneering this approach to higher education?

• • •

My own studies at university and in the years since equipped me with an awareness of the literature in the fields of study most pertinent to the FWC curriculum. Where my knowledge was deficient, I knew how to do the bibliographic research that was needed. I loved this work—immersed in book acquisition, book research, and systematically building up a library to serve a program of world education.

As the books began to fill the shelves that lined the walls around the large open space where chairs and tables were variously arranged for seminars, lectures, presentations, and college community meetings, the feeling of the room took on a new dimension. The variegated size, color, and bindings of the books gave the visual aspect of the room a greater interest. From section to section, multiple points of visual focus emerged as the eye travelled around the walls of the room. A closer look added an intellectual focus to the visual as the categories of books became evident. The acoustics of the room also changed as the walls filled with shelves and the shelves with books. Gone were the hard flat surfaces that bounced sound around the open space. The complex of shapes and textures that now surrounded the space in which presentations, discussion, and conversations took place smoothed out and balanced the acoustic factor in a pleasing way.

Books in a library have multiple uses, one of which is to create an inviting ambiance that draws in patrons and makes them feel comfortably received. It was particularly satisfying to find that in creating a library intended to support the study, research, and learning of students and staff, we were also architecturally appointing a space in a way that had a beneficial subsidiary effect on those who regularly gathered here. These are subtle factors and effects that mostly go unnoticed. No matter, even the unaware are the beneficiaries of these subtle effects, and perhaps that's the way they work best.

• • •

In addition to my library development work at Friends World College, I was tapped to serve in a faculty and student advisor capacity. Because my studies had taken me through concentrations in European intellectual and economic history, East Asian studies, human geography, natural history, and social ecology, I was a good candidate to join Richard Proskauer in representing the field of environmental studies in the college curriculum. Richard was a Harvard PhD in physics and engineering who, in a previous career at the Sperry Rand Corporation, had led the team that developed the oscillating gyroscopic compass. This innovation enabled nuclear submarines to navigate under the sea ice across the North Pole—a journey they could not previously undertake because the compasses with which they were equipped did not work accurately in the polar zone. A change of heart and mind had moved Richard away from working in the military-industrial complex. With his science background, he was now focused on the ecological crisis that unrestrained and unregulated industrial growth was visiting on both the human and natural environments.

Richard came to Friends World College with a unique ability to open eyes. He had a way of seeing and pointing out relationships that conventionally went unnoticed. He made connections and created understandings where before things were blurry and confused and he made pedagogic contributions that went beyond the area of environmental studies. For example, the faculty at the North American Center had a dual role; in addition to being resource persons with regard to the areas of our knowledge, we were expected to assist in the preparation of students for entering the world of cross-cultural experience and learning. Richard's wide ranging interests included anthropology from which he contributed references to three books that offered particularly helpful insights for understanding and engaging with cultures other than one's own: *The Silent Language* by Edward T. Hall (1959), *Freedom and Culture* by Dorothy Lee (1959), and *Stranger and Friend: The Way of an Anthropologist* by Hortense Powdermaker (1966). All three authors were anthropologists.

The Silent Language is especially notable for setting up and laying out examples of misunderstandings and pitfalls that occur when Americans, in particular, live and work in other cultural environments. It was a real gem of a book for inclusion in the college's introduction to cross-cultural experience.

Freedom and Culture is a collection of accessible essays illustrating how the fundamental aspects of social life found in all societies can differ in substantial ways from culture to culture. *Stranger and Friend* is a fieldwork memoir about developing and practicing the skills that enable one to both step into deep engagement with another culture and, when required, step back for assessment. It now seems quite a stretch to think our one semester effort could prepare first year college students for what would come to be successive immersions in different cultures. *The Silent Language*, *Freedom and Culture*, and *Stranger and Friend* became prospective guides for this critical effort.

• • •

Two major books were published in 1962 that helped break through the denial of the environmental crisis: *Silent Spring* by Rachel Carson and *Our Synthetic Environment* by Murray Bookchin (first published under the pen name Lewis Herber). Both books zeroed in on the negative health effects for both humans and the whole commonwealth of life in the widespread use of pesticides in agriculture and general insect eradication, especially mosquitoes. But more than this, both books made clear that the massive and unrestrained dumping of toxic industrial wastes into rivers, lakes, and coastal waters, as well as into the air and landfills, was increasing to such a degree that water, air, and land pollution could now be described without exaggeration as suicidal, or, more accurately, as ecocide. In addition, the introduction of various chemical compounds and non-food elements — many of them synthetic — into industrial food processing were beginning to show up in wide ranging negative health effects in humans and downstream biotic environments. The health and vitality of the whole living world was in decline, earth's life support systems were increasingly compromised, and failing under the impact of toxic pollution and chemical assault.

Rachel Carson was already well known and much loved as a writer on the ecology of coastal environments. Her previous books, *Under the Sea Wind* (1941), *The Sea Around Us* (1951), and *The Edge of the Sea* (1955), were classics of natural history. Her writing was done with a narrative grace and story-telling skill that made her books bestsellers. *Silent Spring* hit the media like a bombshell. For one thing, the title is stunning; it is an unnatural expression of probably the most beloved natural phenomena of life in temperate climates — the coming of the spring season, the reawakening of the green world and the chorus of bird song that accompanies nesting and the bringing forth of new life. The prospect of a silent spring was alarming to a degree that was profoundly shocking.

With one book, Rachel Carson had rung a great bell of warning that got the attention of a wide audience. It started a public policy movement for environmental regulation on the one hand and, on the other, ignited the pushback of the chemical industry and industrial polluters who profited so handsomely from the unrestrained way their products and processes were being deployed in the ever-expanding consumer economy. In the ensuing battles, *Silent Spring* and its allies won the case, and the public policy road to serious and effective environmental regulation began to unfold at the state and federal levels.

Our Synthetic Environment, by Murray Bookchin, was published by Alfred A. Knopf only months before Houghton Mifflin released *Silent Spring*. The timing was unfortunate for Murray. His book on the chemical and industrial pollution threat to human health and the living world is more wide ranging and, in some ways, more deeply grounded in the fundamentals of ecological science than *Silent Spring*. It had been brought out by one of America's most prestigious publishers of serious literary and nonfiction books and was getting good reviews, particularly from biologists, ecologists and science writers. Then came *Silent Spring*. Its publication eclipsed everything else being published on the environmental crisis.

Our Synthetic Environment is written in a heavily researched and detailed style with an underlay of social and economic analysis that probably limited its appeal, and, as Murray later realized and told me, the title is a clunker. Rachel Carson had an awareness of image and the touch of a poet that made her books natural history and literary classics. Portions of *Silent Spring* had already appeared in *The New Yorker*. The bestseller pump was primed and the book went through six printings between May and December of 1962. The Knopf edition of *Our Synthetic Environment* remained in its first printing. It was republished in England in 1975, which indicates that from an editorial view the book had enduring value. In recent years it has been republished several times and is now available online. It was Murray Bookchin's opening act in creating the field of social ecology that he went on to achieve and to which I will return.

•   •   •

Friends World College began operation (1965) in the midst of several cultural battles, including the battle over environmental pollution. A rebirth of the conservation movement was gaining traction and industrial corporations and their financial and political allies were on the defensive. In 1966, Dennis Puleston and a group of conservation colleagues filed a class action suit with the New York Supreme Court against Suffolk County Mosquito Control Commission who, for years, had been spraying DDT over Long Island wetlands. In 1948 Puleston had counted up to three hundred osprey nests on Gardiners Island. By 1966 there were less than fifty nesting pairs of osprey on the island. Dennis knew why. Rachel Carson had implicated DDT toxicity in raptor decline. Dennis analyzed the shells of osprey eggs that had broken under the weight of adult birds instead of hatching. The thin shells were loaded with DDT. In addition the case showed that the famous blue crab was disappearing from The Great South Bay due to DDT poisoning. This caught the attention of influential people, like the judge of the case, who, apparently, was a connoisseur of blue crab. The Suffolk County Legislature banned the further use of DDT.

A year later (1967), Dennis and his allies founded the Environmental Defense Fund (EDF). In 1975 the EDF won the legal battle for a complete nationwide ban on the use of DDT. Had it not been for Dennis Puleston, the raptor population of Long Island, indeed, of the whole of North America might have declined to a point of extinction. In the fall of 1967 Sally Puleston, the daughter of Dennis and Betty Puleston, entered the Friends World College program. I was her faculty advisor for the orientation semester and we have been friends ever since. Two semesters later she was doing photographic work with Jane Goodall at the Gombe Forest chimpanzee study centre in Tanzania. The conservation ethic was in the air and became an important focus for a number of FWC students. It truly fits the bill for the kind of emerging solution to a world problem that Morris Mitchell asked students to make the central part of their study program.

Meanwhile, and germane to the resurgence of the conservation ethos, it was also in 1962 that Lynton K. Caldwell published a seminal paper in the journal, *Public Administration Review* — "Environment: A New Focus for Public Policy." Caldwell was Professor of Government at Indiana University. By 1968, he was acting as a consultant to Senator Henry Jackson who controlled the Senate Interior and Insular Affairs Committee. In this capacity, Caldwell drafted the pioneering document, "A National Policy on the Environment," which became the context for the singular and hugely important National Environmental Policy Act (NEPA), the first legislation of this kind in the world.

Further to this legislation, Lynton Caldwell literally invented the environmental impact assessment process and statement. This critical tool for the development of public environmental policy and the administrative protection of public health and ecosystem integrity has been adopted at the federal, state, and provincial levels across the United States and Canada, and in progressive nations around the world. In 1972, he was instrumental in founding the School of Public and Environmental Affairs at Indiana University, which became an influential centre for research and training in public policy and environmental regulation. Caldwell's success with NEPA and having it passed into law led him to create the National Association of Environmental Professionals (NAEP), a professional association of persons who prepare Environmental Impact Statements. In 2003, his daughter, Elaine Emmi, was a founding member of Quaker Institute for the Future, to which this story will return in the final chapter.

In the fall of 1968 Richard Proskauer attended a meeting of the American Academy of Arts and Sciences in New York City for a major presentation on the environmental crisis and human pollution. The presentation was received with alarm and acclaim, and, as Richard reported it, with the feeling the Rubicon had been crossed. When I met him the next morning on campus he told me "the battle to get the pollution crisis on the public policy agenda is over. The right people now get it." And then, with characteristic foresight, he asked; "What should we be working on next?"

Richard was aware of Kenneth Boulding's "Economics for the Coming Spaceship Earth." He had taken students on field trips to see vast tracts of suburban single-family housing developments overspreading prime Long Island farmland. He had then taken them on a tour of the massive nearby incinerator that received and burned an unbelievable quantity of trash and garbage every day. Action on regulating pollution may have been on the way, but the problem of unlimited economic growth on a finite planet was yet to be recognized. The work of doing environmental education and building up ecological awareness was far from over.

Richard Proskauer was correct in his assessment and forecast. Robert V. Percival writes as follows in the *University of Chicago Legal Forum* (1997):

> During the 1970s, an explosion of federal legislation erected the modern Federal regulatory infrastructure.... The national regulatory legislation that transformed American environmental law during the 1970s was the product of a remarkable groundswell of public concern for the environment. With over-whelming, bipartisan support, this legislation revolutionized US administrative law by...giving citizens access to the courts to ensure that the laws were implemented and enforced.

When it came time for the initial environmental legislation to be reauthorized, the laws were, according to Percival, "broadened, strengthened, and made more specific." As a result, the Safe Drinking Water Act (1984), the Clean Water Act (1986), and the Clean Air Act (1990) became law. Subsequent amendments added regulations and prohibitions on the land disposal of certain hazardous waste. The "cowboy economy" (Kenneth Boulding) of unfettered private action was taking a turn toward the "spaceship economy" of managing throughput for the public good in order to keep the human project from crashing. So far, so good, but as Richard and a growing cadre of ecological thinkers had come to understand, managing pollution by reducing its hazardous risk does not address the environmental breakdown and societal deterioration that the unlimited drive for wealth accumulation is spreading across the earth. This is a new world problem.

The unlimited extraction and processing of natural resources that flows from the drive for unlimited wealth accumulation is a recipe for ecological and societal disaster. Unfortunately, in the hands of transnational corporations and international finance, this has become the *modus operandi* of both capitalist and the so-called socialist economies. They are siblings of the modern era fighting over control of earth's resources at the expense of those who now work hard to survive and the wellbeing of future generations. The intertwining realities of ecological, social, physical, and economic health have been plainly laid out in recent times in such books as *For the Common Good: Redirecting the Economy Toward Community, the Environment, and a Sustainable Future* by Herman Daly and John B. Cobb, Jr. (1989), *Divided Planet: The Ecology of Rich and Poor* by Tom Athanasiou (1996), *The Spirit Level: Why More Equal Societies Almost Always Do Better* by Richard Wilkinson and Kate Pickett (2009), *The Economics of Enough: How to Run the Economy as if the Future Mattered* by Diane Coyle (2011), *Enough is Enough: Building a Sustainable Economy in a World of Finite Resources* by Rob Dietz and Dan O'Neill (2013), and Thomas Picketty's two recent books, *Capital in the Twenty-First Century* (2014) and *Capital and Ideology* (2020).

This is only a small selection of recent and current books in which the authors make the case that our environmental and social crisis, in all its various forms, is rooted in the kind of economic relationships that have come to dominate human adaptation to earth's ecosystems in modern times, and particularly since the advent of hyper-industrialisation and the almost complete financialization of access to the means of life. What is now clear to us about what has gone wrong with the human-earth relationship was just emerging in the mid-60s.

The new environmental and ecological scholarship at the time — both academic and literary — added a complicating dimension to Morris Mitchell's curriculum for Friends World College. The study of world problems and their emerging solutions was now joined by the emergence of a new, and perplexingly fundamental, world problem — the ecologically maladaptive stance the rich nations and regions of the world had taken up in order to increase consumption-based economic growth.

This conundrum of adaptation was not as clear in the mid-60s as it is now, but there is no doubt that a considerable cohort of college age students felt it in their bones and often in their heads as well. There was a shared feeling that something in our society had gone wrong and was continuing to go wrong at an accelerating rate. Friends World College offered a different approach to higher education, an alternative to being processed through a college and university system fully in support of what was going wrong, the most notable examples of which, at the time, were the American war on Vietnam, the violent racism with which the white establishment of the southern states was attempting to suppress the African-American civil rights movement, and the glaring inequity of wealth accumulation and entrenched poverty.

●　　●　　●

Although the college drew on many resource persons for understanding this range of issues and the connections between them, Robert Theobald and Murray Bookchin, in particular, brought especially thoughtful and integrative perspectives to the FWC program.

I had read Robert Theobald's first two books while still in Syracuse and engaged in the study of economics with regard to understanding the persistence of poverty in the midst of growing wealth and abundance. Michael Harrington had published *The Other America* (1962), a study of poverty in the United States that was genuinely shocking and had gotten the attention of more citizens than is usual for a sociology book. In addition, it was showing up in the offices of political leaders. *The Other America* was eventually credited with influencing the Johnson administration's Great Society program.

Robert Theobald published two books in the early 60s that provided an economist's perspective on the relationship between wealth and poverty. *The Rich and the Poor: A Study of the Economics of Rising Expectations* (1960) was written with a global view and from within the dialogue among economists on how to advance economic growth in the poor and "under-developed" regions of the world. *The Challenge of Abundance* (1961) was among the first books to identify the full context of societal change with which the technology and economics of abundance was confronting the rich nations. In addition, Theobald's analysis inserted the moral dimension of human solidarity into a strategy for dealing with poverty.

The context of this dialogue was significantly framed by Walter Rostow with his 1960 publication of *The Stages of Economic Growth: A Noncommunist Manifesto,* in which a theory of "modernization" was embedded that was taken as gospel by economic development economists of the day. In 1963, Robert Heilbroner entered the conversation with the publication of *The Great Ascent,* a title that sounds upbeat but, in fact, was sceptical that the modernization called for by Rostow and company was an inevitable scenario of development that would achieve what they characterized as "economic take off."

Robert Theobald took a different tack. He was hopeful that with the right kind of assistance, the economic wellbeing of nations and regions now struggling with less than adequate subsistence could be improved. However, unlike other economists who saw the route to prosperity as a wholesale conversion to a capitalistic system that exploits resource extraction for the free market economy, Theobald's sensitivity to cultural differences enabled him to think about development in a different way. He approached the development question from the point of view of what makes for healthy and flourishing communities and societies. Clearly, this is a more complex and nuanced issue than simply increasing the gross national product of a country or the average individual income of a region.

It was this cultural perspective that made his books on economic development particularly relevant to the FWC study program. Poverty was certainly one of the world problems on the college's curriculum, but was the bulldozer approach of capitalist modernization the way to create healthy communities?

Was the capitalization of all resources, including human resources, and completely monetizing access to the means of life at the expense of cultural values and norms the way to create secure and flourishing communities and societies? These are big issues that well-informed and culturally aware students need to engage.

Theobald's book, *The Rich and the Poor,* ends with a vision of a new world community coming together to help local communities and regions make decisions about how to use the tools of development for improving access to the means of life in a way that increases the integrity and security of their social and natural environments. *The Challenge of Abundance* includes the call for a new kind of education, an education that includes compassion in the development of intellect and social awareness. The book ends with a chapter titled, "World Citizenship: Dream or Necessity?"

Robert Theobald was born and grew up in India. He did his university work at Cambridge and Harvard and was then employed in both industry and United Nations programs as an economist. In 1963 he published *Free Men and Free Markets,* a book that focuses on the coming impact of the cybernetics revolution and automation on the economies and societies of wealthy nations. He forecast the loss of middle-income jobs and the need for a guaranteed basic income as a matter of social and economic policy. In 1966, he published *The Guaranteed Income: The Next Step in Economic Evolution?* This edited volume was the first comprehensive presentation on the subject. In addition to Theobald's contribution it included essays by Ben Seligman, William Vogt, Erich Fromm, Marshall McLuhan, and Conrad Arensberg, among others. Robert Theobald was living in New York City in the late 60s when I contacted him about participating in the FWC program.

The Guaranteed Income: The Next Step in Economic Evolution? opened the door to what has become an international movement of scholarly research, social policy advocacy, and pilot project implementation. It seemed to me just the kind of emerging solution to the world problem of chronic poverty and the elimination of good paying jobs that automated technology would bring to industrial employment.

Theobald's books dealt with a range of socio-economic issues and displayed a cross-cultural awareness that made them ideal for inclusion in the FWC study program. He was pleased to be asked and eager to contribute in person to a college program that was organized around the study of world problems and their emerging solutions. He was especially responsive to the worldwide, experiential learning component. He was happy to volunteer his time and expertise, which included sharply focused presentations and wide ranging, conversational discussions.

Robert Theobald came back to campus in the late summer of 1970 to participate in consultations that led to structural changes, which enabled Friends World College to continue as an independent institution for another twenty years before becoming part of Long Island University. In addition to its Core Study Program, FWC had developed an Independent Study Program (IPC) component, of which I was the founding coordinator. The IPC arose as a request from students who had developed a particular interest, often geographically based in a country or cultural region, on which they wanted to concentrate. The pedagogic philosophy and practice of the college required that we take these requests into account and adjust the program accordingly. At first the IPC was an ad hoc arrangement, but by 1970 it was clear that it had to be integrated into an overall redesign of FWC's program.

By this time Morris Mitchell had retired from his lead administrative role as president, and the Board of Trustees had appointed Sidney Harmon to this position. Sidney was the co-founder of the Harmon-Kardon Corporation with considerable administrative experience. He had a keen interest in worker-circle management, social justice issues, and educational innovation.[9] With Sidney at the helm in 1970, administrative decisions and fiscal adjustments were made that recognized student requests for extended and/or

---

9   When the Prince Edward County School Board in Virginia closed their entire school system rather than comply with the US Supreme Court decision on school integration, Sidney flew his own plane from Long Island to Virginia several times a week to teach in the schools the African-American community spontaneously organized.

independent study projects as a regular feature of the college's structure. Robert Theobald was especially attentive to these changes and to the innovative significance of the Friends World program. He went on to publish thirteen more books in the next twenty-seven years, each one dealing with some aspect of understanding, coping with, and transforming the trajectories of social, technological, environmental, and economic change into positive outcomes for the future of human communities.

In 1972 he published *Habit and Habitat,* a book in which his perspective and prescription took a decidedly ecological turn. Boulding's warning about infinite growth on a finite planet was sinking in. The famous *Limits to Growth* co-authored by Donella and Dennis Meadows and a team of researchers, was published the same year. Conventional economists tried to laugh it out of town with ridicule, but the thirty-year update published in 2005 more than validated the original analysis. The ridicule has died down because no economist has been able to answer Boulding's challenge. None has even tried; they have just looked the other way. Following Boulding, Herman Daly was one of few economists to pick up the ecological worldview and in 2004, with Joshua Farley, published the textbook of the movement, *Ecological Economics: Principles and Applications.*

Robert Theobald's research, writing, teaching, and consulting continued to develop within this context. Although his perspective took in the larger issues of change and adaptation, he continually returned to the unit of community as the scale of association where people working together can make decisions that build up ecologically coherent, economically secure, and socially flourishing ways of life.

• • •

My association with Murray Bookchin goes back to the Syracuse years as well. I contacted him in New York City after I had seen a reference to his major essay, "Ecology and Revolutionary Thought." He sent me a mimeographed copy. I read it with great interest. Never before had I seen such a comprehensive presentation of cultural history and social analysis so solidly grounded in an ecologically coherent and literate worldview. Then came part two, an even longer essay titled "Towards a Liberatory Technology." Murray Bookchin was no Luddite. This was a man who knew and appreciated the history of technology, who offered a deeply informed critique of its contemporary dehumanizing tendencies, and who had given serious thought, based on extensive knowledge, to how various technologies can be assessed, selected, scaled, and adopted in ways that are truly beneficial for the maintenance of secure and prosperous communities — in short, a human-technology relationship in which tools function to serve social and ecological integrity and wellbeing.

I had by this time read a lot of the emerging environmental and ecological literature. My background in cultural history, human geography, and economics gave me a grounding in social dynamics, power relationships, and in the patterns of environmental settlement and livelihood adaptations. Murray Bookchin's two essays brought the realms of earth's ecological reality and human social development into a parallel and interacting focus in a remarkable and truly original way. Nothing I had previously read achieved this unity of insight into the governing dynamics of the human-earth relationship. Murray's integration of social and ecological understanding, along with a visionary, yet nuts and bolts, scenario for the re-adaptation of human settlements in ecologically sound, socially secure, and economically sustainable ways was truly unique.

Lewis Mumford had been my guide to understanding the history of technology and human adaptation. Murray Bookchin now provided a dimension of social insight grounded in ecology and the earth sciences that moved scholarship to activism. One could read Mumford and come to understand the kind of public policy and institutional changes needed to help steer industrial-consumer civilization away from ecological and social catastrophe. One could read Bookchin and understand what to do — how to become active both socially and ecologically — to help "create a new society within the shell of the old," as Peter

Maurin, founder of the Catholic Worker Movement with Dorothy Day, had succinctly framed the task.

Murray had already written and published a major book on the environmental crisis, as previously noted. He was now well on the way to formulating and articulating a new synthesis of social and ecological analysis and a new discipline of scholarship, along with activist guidelines for reconstructing both social and ecological relationships. He gave this new context of analysis, study, and action the name "social ecology," being careful to distinguish it from the way sociology might use the term to simply characterize the network of relationships within various dimensions of society.

Social ecology, in the usage defined by Murray Bookchin, meant a fused understanding and reciprocal mirroring of human social relationships and human-earth relationships within the governing context of planetary life support systems. Dysfunctional and destructive relationships within the social realm are mirrored in the human-earth relationship. Traditions of hierarchy, domination, and marginalization entrenched in human social relationship are the same behavioural dynamics that are wrecking the human-earth relationship. Social ecology as a discipline, as a lens of understanding that embeds human behaviour within earth process, is a distinct and unique contribution to the ecological worldview.

When we relocated to Long Island and joined the staff of Friends World College, contacting Murray about providing seminar presentations and discussions for groups of students was on my agenda. But an enthusiastic student beat me to it. I was using Murray's two essays as collateral reading for environmental studies. Roger Mann was inspired to contact the author and arrange to meet with him at his apartment just off Washington Square in Manhattan.

Murray welcomed the opportunity and assumed the role of providing introductory seminars on cultural history and social ecology. We would journey to the city for evening sessions with Murray, which were somewhat open-ended. He had a highly disciplined mind, but his approach was to play his presentations and lead discussions off the thoughts, questions, and concerns that students brought to the meetings. A better fit with Friends World pedagogy would be hard to imagine.

Murray was a charismatic figure and enjoyed holding court, but at the same time came across as a kind of rumpled uncle with whom one felt immediately comfortable. He paid close attention to the contributions students brought to the meetings and made distinct efforts to help them formulate and articulate their thoughts and questions.

I remember one evening in particular when the discussion turned to the differences between various cultures. Murray was attuned to the cross-cultural, educational odyssey these students were about to undertake. In sharing what he knew and had experienced, he launched into a kind of rhapsody about the "essential domesticity" of Arabic culture. I remember the way he cupped his hands and lifted them to eye level as he spoke. The gesture had intensity about it, giving the impression of symbolically sheltering and honouring something precious and even sacred that informed his discourse. He expanded on the ethos of mutual support that characterized the social relationships of traditional village and communal life. In his description, the aura of domesticity radiated from the household to encompass village life and secure a sense of communal solidarity.

In another instance, when he was illustrating how to understand the complexity of the industrial-consumer economy and the commodities it produces, he spontaneously picked up a pack of cigarettes someone had left laying on the table and, layer-by-layer, peeled back the components and processes by which it had been assembled. It was a remarkable exercise of reverse engineering that illustrated so well the networks of relationship and coordinated processes that go into making even the simplest of commodities. Murray was a great teacher, and by attending his seminars we learned not just what he had to teach, but a good deal about how to teach as well.

For all his erudition, Murray was not a credentialed academic. He certainly could have been, but, in fact, he had no need of such a pedigree. He was a working class intellectual, although he would likely reject the label because he came ultimately to reject the utility of class designations. He was born into and grew up in a Marxist family, but educated himself into a position of commanding breadth with regard to cultural history and the trajectories and prospects of social change movements. He often railed against hardcore Marxists for their fundamentalist mindset and inflexibility. Among other employments, Murray had been an autoworker, a union organizer, and a longshoreman.

Murray seemed primed with a kind of perpetual ebullience, a kind of alertness that was interested in almost everything. He responded to students with his own learning antenna fully deployed. I remember one night after the seminar we all walked over to the Filmore East near Second Avenue and 106th Street to catch the tail end of a rock concert. Murray was in his element as we sauntered along. He cracked jokes and engaged with the students like he was a peer and they returned the attention. In those days we had a term for this kind of association; it was called an "affinity group." The group affinity with Murray was necessarily fluid because students were passing through on their way to a world education, but it was real and touching, and, for me and a few others, long lasting.

At this time Murray had yet to publish his social ecology writings in book form. We circulated the essays we already had and the new ones he shared with us. But I was a college librarian, a worker in the commonwealth of books, and I wanted good solid volumes to put on the shelves to which I could direct students and my fellow faculty members. At one point, I asked Bea (Beatrice), his wife, about the prospects for book publication. She told me Murray was working on a book of cultural history, political philosophy, and social ecology that would bear comparison with Marcuse's *Eros and Civilization*, except, she added, it will be a more comprehensive and better balanced work of analysis and synthesis. It would be titled *The Ecology of Freedom: The Emergence and Dissolution of Hierarchy*. I was glad to hear this. Bea said he had been working on it for years and it was hard to say when it would be ready to publish. I thought, OK, it will be worth the wait. This will be a book for the ages, not just the moment.

As it turned out, *The Ecology of Freedom* was not published until 1982, fourteen years later. A second edition was released in 1991, which was republished in 2005. The book has enjoyed an enduring presence and has been highly influential in the field of contemporary ecological studies. One the one hand, it has had the effect of putting ecologists on notice that their life system and earth science studies have a social and cultural dimension of profound importance for the future of the human project. On the other hand, it has defined social ecology as a comprehensive narrative and coherent worldview in which the human-earth relationship can be helpfully understood and serve as the basis for intelligent and resilient ecosystem adaptation.

Murray's book publishing history, however, begins almost a decade earlier, though not early enough for me to start a Bookchin collection for the library at Friends World College. In 1974, while teaching in the Social Ecology Studies program at Goddard College in Vermont, he published *The Limits of the City*. In 1977 he finished and published *The Spanish Anarchists*. In 1982, Murray's book publishing began to take off. In addition to *The Ecology of Freedom*, he published a collection of essays titled *Toward an Ecological Society*. In 1986 he published two more books: *The Modern Crisis* and *Post-Scarcity Anarchism*. The list goes on: *The Rise of Urbanization and the Decline of Citizenship* (1987), *Remaking Society* (1989), *The Philosophy of Social Ecology* (1990), *Defending the Earth* (1991), *Social Anarchism or Lifestyle Anarchism: An Unbridgeable Chasm* (1995), *The Murray Bookchin Reader* (1997), and *Social Ecology and Communalism* (2007). This last book was published after Murray's death in 2006, but he prepared it as a final testament. It's particularly important because it reiterates the foundation in communal life of his social philosophy and activism.

At the 20th anniversary reunion of Friends World College I learned that Murray's connection with the college had continued through the initiative of students who picked up the link. In addition, and to my amazement, I learned he had been invited to be the commencement speaker at a graduation ceremony. Had I known about this in advance, I might have travelled from our home in Canada to Long Island to relish the event and be touched once again by the sense of affinity that graced my association with Murray Bookchin.

• • •

The time came when I had to deal with the flood of donated books that had been sent to the administrative headquarters of Friends World College at Harrow Hill. Harrow Hill is a modest estate — as such things go on Long Island — set on ten acres of nicely managed lawns and woods at Muttontown, a nostalgically named community midway between Westbury and Cold Spring Harbor in north central Nassau County. By 1963 the Committee on a Friends World College had gathered enough dedicated volunteers and financial resources to begin making concrete plans toward the realization of its vision. The Committee had become increasingly successful in developing a wide-ranging support base. As with many Quaker projects, support from people who were not members of the Society of Friends became critically important. Among contributions received was the Harrow Hill estate, donated by Henry Ittleson, a New York banker and philanthropist. This property provided the facilities for an administrative base and became the setting for a pilot project in the summer of 1963. Under the name of Friends World Institute, an international, cross cultural mix of students were assembled at Harrow Hill and, directed by Harold Taylor, began an experimental exploration of world oriented education.[10]

When the call went out to supporters of the FWC project for book donations with which to start the college library, it must have struck a double chord of response; an aging generation of good hearted, book collecting Quakers and their fellow travellers were moved by the opportunity to help the college project and, at

---

10 An account of this project, written by Harold Taylor, appeared in the November 14, 1964 issue of *The Saturday Review* under the title. "The Idea of a World College."

the same time, clean out their aging collections of once relevant books that now gathered dust on their library shelves. The idea of sparing their adult children the burden of dealing with their books likely appealed, or it may have been the adult children themselves who seized the opportunity to start dealing with their parent's accumulated books.

In any event, the books arrived at Harrow Hill in such volume that there was nothing for it but to stash carton after carton in the basement of the main house. Most of this had occurred before I arrived as the college librarian. When I was shown the accumulation, which was described to me as a treasure trove of books waiting to be liberated from their boxes and organized on the shelves of the college library, I stifled my reaction. I had been a worker in the commonwealth of books long enough to know that what I was viewing was more of a problem than a boon. I opened a few boxes and could immediately see that only a fraction of the donated books would be appropriate for adding to the college's library.

First, for the most part, they were marked by their era of publication. Second, the basement, where all this evidence of liberal generosity was stored, was noticeably damp. The boxes on the bottom of the jumble-like pile, stacked head high, were structurally deteriorating and showing signs of mold. Dealing with this lot did not rise to the top of my agenda. I had a $10,000 budget with which to target the purchase of current, topflight books, keyed especially to the college curriculum and the interests of students.

But the time came when these donated books had to be dealt with. The founding committee saw Harrow Hill as the site on which to develop the college campus but this anticipation ran afoul of Muttontown zoning, which for that area was residential only. When this was discovered, a site for a temporary campus was negotiated with Nassau County. Mitchel Air Force Base, now abandoned, stood adjacent to the town of Westbury. Part of the property had been converted to other uses, but Nassau County still retained ownership of the officer's residence compound, called

Mitchel Gardens, that stood on a wedge of land between Stewart Avenue and the backside of Roosevelt Raceway. The facility included two-dozen single-story duplex housing units and a large dining hall with a fully equipped kitchen. The site had been abandoned for some years but had been well built and, with clean-up and appropriate renovations, was ready for re-occupancy. The property and buildings were leased to Friends World College by Nassau County for a dollar a year, and so became the North American Center of the new institution for the first five years of operation.

Then, like a fairy godmother, Eleanor Hoffman Rodewald Livingston, the widow of Gerald Moncrieffe Livingston, once a Governor of the New York Stock Exchange, made her ninety-three acre estate at Lloyd Harbor on Long Island's North Shore available to the college. She had homes in Connecticut and the Bahamas and the Livingston Estate at Lloyd Harbor was now mostly unused. The arrangement was essentially a donation with a token payment of $100,000. The property included four residences in addition to the manor house, a big barn, a boathouse big enough and rigged up to accommodate a good sized schooner, a large greenhouse, formal gardens now gone wild, and a free standing ballroom equipped with a stage and dressing rooms. The manor house was of pre-Revolutionary War vintage and, we were told, had been shelled by a British ship from Lloyd Harbor. It had doorways and ceilings that caused you to realize people were considerably shorter in those days.

The property also came with Henry Scutter, an ancient personage who lived in what must have been the cook's residence, which stood just a few steps from the backdoor of the manor house kitchen. The place came with Henry and Henry came with a story. The word was, Henry had once been a Long Island fisherman. Through some misfortune, his boat sank in Lloyd Harbor, he came ashore on the Livingston Estate, and had been there ever since. He must have found a niche as a kind of handyman, but by the time Friends World College took over he was mostly a storyteller, although he did show me how to spot the holes at low tide where clams are buried and how to properly gather eelgrass for mulching.

And, finally, with the acquisition of the Livingston Estate, Friends World College came into possession of a recently abandoned Nike missile base. On the property's flat hilltop, well away from the waterfront buildings of the estate, the Pentagon had located one of the missile launching sites with which it had ringed New York City in the Cold War era. The first generation Nike missiles installed at these sites were set up to take down Russian bombers should they be sent to attack the City. The missiles were long gone but the silos were still there along with a cluster of cement block buildings that proved quite serviceable when the college relocated to the Livingston estate. The college library that I had curated to include the best literature available on peace studies and the nonviolent resolution of conflict was eventually located in the missile base's main building. The irony was not lost on us. Twice in the short life of this Quaker inspired college we had serendipitously become the beneficiary of the US military's abandoned infrastructure. The nuance of the case, however, could also be turned the other way around. We could see the occupancy of these facilities for the purpose of advancing cross-cultural understanding and world peace as "beating swords into ploughshares."

Once the Livingston Estate was secured as the future headquarters and North American campus of Friends World College, Harrow Hill could be sold, which meant all the books stored in the basement had to be cleared out and transported to the college's future home. The ballroom building was our staging site. The boxes of books were hauled, load after load, from the basement of Harrow Hill to Livingston and restacked at the front of the ballroom. Tables were set up in the middle of the ballroom floor and preliminary sorting began. Meanwhile, the summer room wing of the manor house, which had screened full-length windows on three sides and a stone floor, was cleared out and filled with multiple rows of metal shelving. The task was to do a four stage sorting: 1) cull and discard the books that had been damaged by dampness and mildew or were otherwise of no value; 2) separate and re-box the books that were unsuitable for a college library but might be of interest to used book dealers; 3) spot the books that were relevant for adding to the current library at the Mitchel Gardens campus; and 4) transfer the books that had some prospect of being retained for inclusion in a larger library to the metal shelves in the summer room. The bulk of the books were transferred to this location where they could be seen and further evaluated.

An amazing number of copies of the same titles had been donated. This could have been predicted, but, of course, there would be no way to prevent it. It was an interesting exercise; you could see the titles, decade after decade, starting in the 20s and 30s and coming up through the 50s that had been best sellers to the demographic that had responded to the request for book donations. The repeating titles ranged from books of popular history (a lot of Winston Churchill), to biographies and memoirs of political figures, to books concerned with international relations and war and peace issues, accounts of international travel and adventure, the works of famous journalists, literary bestsellers of the eras, and strange to say, or perhaps not so strange, handyman manuals on building, fixing, and taking care of things around the house and homestead.

Occasionally, in the midst of the slog through so many unpromising and redundant books, surprising titles came to light; for example a matching set of Henry Miller's *Tropic of Cancer* and *Tropic of Capricorn* published by Obelisk Press in Paris (1948 editions), a 1927 Nonesuch Press edition of *Pencil Drawings by William Blake* edited by Geoffrey Keynes and printed at Chiswick Press in England, and a 1941 reprint of a 1919 Alfred A. Knopf edition of *Translations from the Chinese* by Arthur Waley illustrated by Cyrus LeRoy Baldridge. A splendid technical note at the back of this handsome collection of classic Chinese poetry provides an image of how fine editions were made in those days.

> This volume, illustrated and decorated by Cyrus LeRoy Baldridge, was planned by Richard Ellis and produced under his direction. It was composed in

a special Monotype cutting of Frederic W. Goudy's Deepdene type made for this edition, with swash letters and revised characters designed by Mr Ellis with the approval of Mr Goudy.

The paper, patterned after old papers of the orient, was manufactured by the P. H. Glatfelter Company, Spring Grove, Pennsylvania. The full-color illustrations were reproduced in Similetone by the Zeese-Wilkinson Company, Long Island City, New York. The cloth, in a natural finish, was made by Bancroft Mills, Wilmington, Delaware. The composition, Electrotyping, Printing and Binding were by The Haddon Craftsmen, Camden, New Jersey.

That's the way to make a fine book—local and regional production all the way through.

Finally, with the damaged and unusable books disposed of and the remainder out on shelves where they could eventually be sorted with sober second thought, the task of dealing with the donated books was behind me for the time being. As it turned out that task was behind me for good. My work as an acquisitions librarian, along with other requirements met by curriculum and program development, had satisfied the New York State Board of Regents and Friends World was granted its Liberal Arts College Charter.

•　　•　　•

In the summer of 1969, Ellen and I were asked if we would go to Kenya to help run the FWC East African Center. A new director from Kenya had been hired and the American couple that had been on staff was returning home. The Center, which had been operating out of a large rented house in Nairobi, had been moved to a facility called Kaptagat Arms located in the rural highlands two-hundred miles northwest of Nairobi. This was an unforeseen opportunity, and we said, "Yes." I expected that would be the end of my library work for a while, but that's not the way our East African sojourn turned out.

Kaptagat Arms, as the name indicates, was a facility leftover from the British colonial era. It was a rustic resort complex built to provide British civil servants and their families a vacation spot within East Africa and accommodate important guests from the "Mother Country." At an elevation of 7500 feet, the area was free of malaria carrying mosquitoes and poisonous snakes. The nights were cool and the days pleasantly warm. We were thirty miles from the Equator, but during the long rainy season enjoyed laying a fire in the fireplace with which our small cottage was equipped.

Since the end of British rule in Kenya, its use had declined and the property was for sale at a bargain price. Friends World College bought it and now had an East African Center that comfortably accommodated students and staff in small cottages and in a single story hotel-like building. The central lodge looked like something that had been imported from the Adirondacks or the Maine Woods. The interior was finished in dark wood with a cathedral ceiling over a lounge area with a large stone fireplace. The heads of wild animals mounted on decorative plaques flanked the fireplace and circled the room on three sides. The British administration and their great white hunters had left their mementoes of conquest in place.

Even more disconcerting than having an old missile base in your backyard was to hold meetings with students under the long dead gaze of large animals killed for sport. The students, to a person, would undoubtedly have come down on the side of animal rights and wildlife protection. Friends World, a Quaker sponsored college, was developing a track record of repurposing incongruous facilities—first, a World War Two military housing compound, then a Cold War missile installation site, and now a British Colonial era resort with a big game hunting heritage. And, to top it off, the purchase included an agreement to retain the current employees of Kaptagat Arms, which included a night watchman who carried a gun in his overcoat pocket.

As might have been expected, but much to my surprise, Kaptagat Arms was equipped with a real library. I knew the books that had been a resource at the Nairobi house had been brought to Kaptagat, but I had no idea that a fully appointed library room was attached to the manager's residence. The room had lovely built-in shelves, a library desk, a study table, and a dictionary stand. It looked like something right out of an English country home. It was so well organized it even had a card catalogue with a self-serve book checkout system. The books in the collection, which had come with the property, were mostly classics of English literature. In addition there were books on East African travel and natural history, along with narratives of big game hunting and other adventure stories, some from the early days of European exploration in Africa. What it lacked was books about contemporary East Africa: books about culture, politics, economics, sociology, geography, agriculture, education, health and social support systems, ecology and wildlife research—all the areas of study the FWC curriculum took into account.

There was plenty of shelf room, there were a couple of bookstores in Nairobi that looked promising, and the Center had a budget for program resources. The furloughed librarian was back in business—part time and small scale, but definitely a man with a mission. A book person is like a border collie. If a border collie doesn't have sheep to herd, it will herd chickens or children or whatever moves that comes within its notice, and border collies notice everything that moves. A book person notices and tends to herd up books wherever they are. Some are lucky enough to be employed as full time book herders, like a border collie on a sheep farm. If otherwise employed, a book person will herd up his or her own library collection and visit bookstores at every opportunity.

Librarian was still in my job description and book herding was still my instinct. Rounding up pertinent books to background and supplement the experiential learning opportunities offered to students by the Friends World East Africa Program was as natural to me as it is for a border collie to bring in the sheep for the night. All we need is a signal, and off we go on our mission. The library room at Kaptagat Arms was my signal.

My mission, in this regard, converged on two bookstores in Nairobi and tracking down bookstores in Mombasa and Kampala when we travelled to the Kenyan coast and Uganda. I also discovered that a tourist merchandise shop in the international airport at Entebbe had an excellent selection of books on East Africa.

The two bookstores in Nairobi were an interesting contrast. The one that proved the most useful to me was located a short distance from the New Stanley Hotel in the central business district. It was definitely of colonial heritage. Once inside you could easily imagine you had just stepped off a street in Cambridge or Oxford.

The other bookstore was some distance from the New Stanley in a commercial district where Indian families were the shopkeepers. It was part stationery supplies and part bookstore. The books were spread out like a supermarket display and were a potpourri of offerings from and for the cultural mix that made up Nairobi: African, Indian, and English. Between these two bookstores and others I found as we conducted study-travel programs around East Africa, I assembled a decent collection of useful books on both recent regional history and contemporary cultural, social, political, economic, and environmental topics.

•　　•　　•

In 1969 it was only five years since Britain had been forced to concede to the independence movement and a Kenyan government had replaced the colonial administration. But the English and Indian populations had been here for generations and the colonial heritage was still very much in evidence. Indian shopkeepers still dominated the commercial trade in Nairobi and in much of Kenya, but the move was on to drive them out to make room for African entrepreneurs. When we left Kenya, our Libyan Airlines flight to London was packed with Indian families carrying all manner of personal and household goods, including rolled up rugs.

As citizens of the Commonwealth they held British passports and without barrier could seek refuge in England.

In 1969, politics and political conflict dominated Kenyan life. It was a one-party system in which aspiring political leaders carved out opposition movements within the party. Jomo Kenyatta, who had led the fight for independence, was the first president and was now up for re-election. Tom Mboya, a prominent and fast rising political leader, had been assassinated on a downtown Nairobi street two weeks before we landed in the city. Violent protest demonstrations had flared up around the country. Oginga Odinga, Kenya's first vice president and now Kenyatta's main rival was arrested and jailed soon after we arrived. He remained in prison for two years. In the fall of 1969, Kenyatta campaigned for re-election. When he came to a rally in Eldoret (a large town near Kaptagat), he spoke to the crowd from behind a bulletproof plexiglass enclosure. If you were interested in politics and how democracy was faring as an emerging concept around the world, there was plenty to study in East Africa.

A good place to start is the book *Facing Mount Kenya*, an anthropological study of the Gikuyu people that Kenyatta had written and published in 1938 as a student at the London School of Economics. Since I had not yet read it, I brought a copy of the American edition with me and added it to the FWC Center library. The Gikuyu people are the largest ethnic group in Kenya, and, although only 17% of the total population, regard themselves as the natural leaders of the country. With that in mind, and with Gikuyu tradition of "big man" leadership, political life in Kenya was evolving in fraught ways. The whole East African political and cultural development scene, which included the figures of Julius Nyerere in Tanzania and Milton Obote in Uganda, was an emerging phenomenon in 1969, and I collected the books for the FWC library that documented it. In 1967, Oginga Odinga published *Not Yet Uhuru*, which is a biographical and historical account of the struggle for freedom (uhuru) from British rule and a blistering attack on Kenyatta for having become an "imperialist stooge" and betraying the uhuru movement.

The scene in Tanzania was different. Nyerere rose to the challenge of uniting the ethnic diversity of the country by anchoring a political philosophy he called "African socialism" in the customs and institutions of family kinship and village life based on mutual support and solidarity. In 1968, he published, *Ujamaa: Essays on Socialism*. Ujamaa is a Kiswahili word that means "extended family;" it asserts that a person becomes a person through the people or community. It identifies the spirit of being with others, being in community, of bringing groups of families together, and in "fostering cohesion, love, and service." Nyerere's book was a primary text for understanding his effort to bring a fundamental reality of African social life into an emerging ethos for the development and governance of his country. He was adamant that African socialism owed nothing to European socialism. It did not emerge from a sense of competition with capitalism. It emerged from a fundamental and pervasive African ethos of family, village, and tribal life—a unique African contribution to human development. A 1967 essay by Nyerere ends with these words.

> We, in Africa, have no more need of being 'converted' to socialism than we have of being 'taught' democracy. Both are rooted in our own past—in the traditional society which produced us. Modern African socialism can draw from its traditional heritage the recognition of 'society' as an extension of the basic family within the limits of the tribe, or, indeed, of the nation. For no true African socialist can look at a line drawn on a map and say. 'The people on this side of that line are my brothers, but those who happen to live on the other side of it can have no claim on me'; every individual on this continent is his brother.

> It was in the struggle to break the grip of colonialism that we learnt the need for unity. We came to recognize that the same socialist attitude of mind

which, in the tribal days, gave to every individual the security that comes of belonging to a widely extended family, must be preserved within the still wider society of the nation. But we should not stop there. Our recognition of the family to which we all belong must be extended yet further — beyond the tribe, the community, the nation, or even the continent — to embrace the whole society of mankind. This is the only logical conclusion for true socialism.[11]

Here was rich ground for studying a social and cultural situation emerging into a larger political reality. It seemed tailor made for Morris Mitchell's vision of what would come into view for students launched on a program of world education.

Uganda gained its independence from Britain two years earlier than Kenya and was governed by the Uganda People's Congress, a political party led by Milton Obote from 1962 to 1971. The new government started out as a parliamentary system but was converted to a unitary presidential system by Obote as he con-solidated political power. Obote, too, had a vision of African socialism, but unlike Nyerere, he moved more and more to an autocratic leadership style. In his attempt to shape Uganda into a democratic republic, Obote was faced with several large tribal configurations that were traditionally ruled by a privileged caste of leaders who had accommodated to colonial rule in ways that ensured their continued hold on wealth and power.

These tribal leaders opposed the loss of their status that would come with the implementation of Obote's philosophy of government for Uganda. He characterized these tribal configurations as "feudalism" and the tribal leaders as repressive "overlords" determined to preserve their wealth and privilege. The conflict turned violent and Obote used military force to repress and defeat his political enemies, which he justified by insisting that unitary governance and centralized social and

---

11   https://www.jpanafrican.org/edocs/e-DocUjamma3.5.pdf

economic policies would benefit "the common man" and enable Uganda to become an increasingly more equitable, prosperous, and secure nation.

By 1969, the Uganda People's Congress was firmly in power and Milton Obote began publishing a series of pamphlets that spelled out his grand vision for the political and economic development of the country. The first and primary document was titled *The Common Man's Charter*, which was approved by an Annual Delegates Conference of the Uganda People's Congress. A second publication titled, *The Move to the Left*, spelled out steps for implementing the *Charter*. These documents expressed Obote's vision of African Socialism for Uganda in highly sophisticated language. They were clearly the product of having thoroughly grasped the potential of democratic socialism in both philosophical and policy dimensions. For example, *The Common Man's Charter* begins as follows:

> We hereby commit ourselves to create in Uganda conditions of full security, justice, equality, liberty and welfare for all sons and daughters of the Republic of Uganda and for the realisation of those goals we have adopted the Move to the Left Strategy ... We subscribe fully to Uganda always being a Republic and have adopted this Charter so that the implementation of this Strategy prevents effectively any one person or group of persons from being masters of all or a section of the people of Uganda, and ensure that all citizens of Uganda become truly masters of their own destiny.

The Charter further defines the new political reality of the nation:

> Republicanism in Uganda, just like the political Independence of Uganda, is now a reality, but the demand and struggle for Uhuru has no end. ... the people of Uganda must move away from the ways and

mental attitudes of the colonial past, move away from the hold of tribal and other forms of factionalism and the power of vested interests, and accept that the problems of poverty, development and nation-building can and must be tackled on the basis of one Country and one People. ... The feudalists wanted to continue to rule as they used to before the coming of the British and they did not want the common man to have a say in the shaping of the destiny of an independent Uganda. ... That situation, however, is no longer with us. Uganda is now a Republic. ... Thus, the reason for this Charter. ... With the removal of the feudal factor from our political and economic life, we need to do two things. First we must not allow the previous position of the feudalists to be filled by neo-feudalists. Secondly, we must move away from circumstances which may give birth to neo-feudalism or generate feudalistic mentality. The move to the Left is the creation of a new political culture and a new way of life, whereby the people of Uganda as a whole — their welfare and their voice in the National Government and in other local authorities — are paramount.[12]

The *Charter* goes on at great length to explain the philosophy of government and the accompanying policies the Uganda People's Congress intends to follow and put in place for the benefit of all citizens and the country as a whole.

We were in Uganda with a group of students on a study-travel project when *The Common Man's Charter* was published. It was headline news around the country. When we arrived back in Kampala, I obtained several copies from the government printing

---

12 https://web.archive.org/web/20110727195757/http://www.
    radiorhino.org/htm_material/archiv/text/press/monitor/
    THE%20COMMON%20MAN%20CHARTER%20By%20
    DrAMO.htm

office. On returning to Kaptagat, I added them to our library's growing collection of books and papers on the political and socio-economic development taking place in the three countries of the region. I later obtained *The Move to the Left* as well. With a growing collection of primary documents at hand reflecting the contrasting approaches of Kenya, Tanzania, and Uganda to political, economic, and social development, students at the East African Center of Friends World College were face to face in real-time with a major world problem—de-colonization and its various emerging solutions.

The reality of independence was accompanied by the fact that the colonial masters had imposed the geography and admin-istration of nation states on the highly varied ethnic and tribal geography of East Africa. Kenya was made up of forty-two tribes, Uganda was composed of fifty-four tribes, and Tanzania encompassed more than one hundred and twenty tribes. Nyerere was attempting to inspire a national commitment to the common good based on the reality of kinship and the solidarity of village life. Kenyatta, according to his critics, had succumbed to the "big man" political ethos and, with his followers, simply stepped into the administrative and economic structures that colonialism had erected and left behind. Obote was determined to check and eliminate the colonial and pre-colonial structures of social and economic exploitation of people and resources that were still in place at the time of independence.

After independence, all three governments moved toward one-party political systems: Obote, with a deliberate and well articulated pan-ethnic rationale; Kenyatta, with a "father of the nation" image and the intimidating dominance of his Gikuyu tribe; Nyerere, with moral suasion around cooperation for the common good. It would be hard to imagine a better context for learning about the problem of colonization that European powers foisted on various regions of the world, or for studying the similarities, contrasts, and complexities of the political, social, and economic responses to "national" independence and the fraught process of de-colonization.

• • •

Another door to world education — one that a librarian is especially well positioned to open — is the literary heritage of each cultural region of the planet.

Literary heritage has two dimensions: the accumulated heritage of story-telling from the past and the ongoing contribution of story-telling being created in the present. While the heritages of story-telling that have been recorded from the various traditions of world literature are a rich tapestry, it is the unfolding heritage of story-telling in the form of contemporary novels, short stories, poetry, and essays that provide access to the immediacy of what is happening in a cultural region. Some students respond with interest to the primary documents of a region's political, economic, social, and environmental issues, but the contemporary literary work of a cultural region often catches the imagination in a more vital way and offers a more accessible path into cross-cultural learning.

Contemporary African literature was rapidly developing in the late 60s. It had first come to my attention when I was managing the Syracuse Book Center. Heinemann, a UK publisher dating from the 1890s, initiated its African Writers Series in 1962 with the release of *Things Fall Apart* by Chinua Achebe and *Burning Grass* by Cyprian Ekwensi. In 1963 they published Achebe's *No Longer at Ease* and Ekwensi's *People of the City*. In 1964 they published six more titles, including *Weep Not Child* by James Ngugi and *Zambia Shall Be Free* by Kenneth Kaunda. The series was off and running and I established an African Literature section at the Syracuse Book Center.

By 1969 — the year we came to East Africa — the contemporary literary heritage of the continent was rapidly developing; fifty-eight titles had been published in Heinemann's African Writers Series. I had added several of the titles to the Friends World College library at the North American Center, but I now had the opportunity to bring contemporary African literature to the attention of students at the East African Center. The British-style bookstore in Nairobi was well stocked with the African Writers Series. The books were being produced and promoted for use in educational programs and were suitably printed in uniform, low cost, paperback editions. This made it possible, within my modest budget, to assemble a core selection of the most pertinent books from the series for the East African Center library. In addition to the titles already noted, my selection included *The River Between*, *A Grain of Wheat*, and *The Black Hermit* by James Ngugi, *The Arrow of God* and *A Man of the People* by Chinua Achebe, *Mine Boy* by Peter Abrahams, *Lokotown and Other Stories* by Cyprian Ekwensi, *Child of Two Worlds* by Mugo Gatheru, *The Only Son* by John Munonye, *No Easy Task* by Aubrey Kachingwe, *Efuru* by Flora Nwapa, *Houseboy* and *The Old Man and the Medal* by Ferdinand Oyono, *One Man, One Wife* and *Kinsman and Foreman* by T. M. Aluko, *A Woman in Her Prime* by Asare Konadu, *The Beautiful Ones Are Not Yet Born* by Ayi Kwei Armah, *Dying in the Sun* by Peter K. Serumaga, *Return to the Shadows* by Robert Serumaga, *Not Yet Uhuru* by Oginga Odinga, *Neo-Colonialism: The Last Stage of Imperialism* by Kwame Nkrumah, *On Trial for My Country* by Stanlake Samkange, and several anthologies of African literature, including *Origin East Africa* edited by David Cook, *Modern African Prose* edited by Richard Rive, and *A Book of African Verse* edited by John Reed and Clive Wake.

Following the lead of Heinemann, East African Publishing House was established in 1965 in partnership with Andre Deutsch. Andre Deutsch later pulled out and EAPH became the first book publishing business wholly owned and operating in East Africa. EAPH began their Modern African Library series with the publication of *The Promised Land* and *Land Without Thunder* by Grace Ogot and *Song of Lawino* and *Song of Ocol* by Okot p'Bitek, all of which I added to the FWC library at Kaptagat. As diverse as all this flourishing of creative writing came to be, there was an underlying sense of dislocation and an overarching response of struggle in almost all it. The ghost of colonial disruption haunts this literature and the conflicts that are rampant in the effort to re-establish authentic African identities—both personal and cultural—appear in various ways in almost every narrative.

Books like *Wretched of the Earth* and *Black Skin, White Masks* by Frantz Fanon and *The Colonizer and the Colonized* by Albert Memmi provide a deep dive into the psychodynamics of colonization and the cultural effects that result from both overt and covert domination. But it has been the novels, short stories, plays, poetry, and memoirs of this first generation of post-colonial African writers that provide the textures and colors, the frustration and heartbreak, the panorama of lived experience that came to the people as the domination of colonialism descended and as neo-colonialism now emerges. These books are not just historical documents, but continue to testify to the kind of cultural dislocation, personal and social upheaval, political conflicts, and environmental disruption that still plague the world as the result of European colonialism and its aftermath.

In addition to having this literature at hand, I had the opportunity to make contact with two authors and incorporate meetings with them into FWC's East African program. At one point on a Uganda study trip, we discovered that Kenyan writer Ngũgĩ wa Thiong'o was scheduled to give a lecture at Makerere University in Kampala on contemporary African writing and African identity. By this time he had already published three novels and had become a leading voice among African writers. He was also still using the name James Ngugi. He later took his full Gikuyu name, a move that was foreshadowed in his Makerere lecture in 1970.

He spoke about the fact that writing in English and achieving success as an African writer was not congruent with the full realization of an African identity. In both a personal sense and in the context of developing an authentic African literature, the modes of thinking, the structures of concepts, the ways of expressing relationships and the processes of life in English were not congruent with his African experience and language. He didn't offer a programmatic answer to this dilemma but rather raised and explored the conundrum for his academic audience. Later in his career, he stopped writing in English and began to write in Gikuyu. He developed a program of Gikuyu language publications.

He was willing for his work to be translated into English, but his concern became focused on the preservation of his African language and the creation of authentic literature for his people that enhanced their cultural identity.

Sheldon Weeks, an American teaching at Makerere University, arranged a meeting with Ngũgĩ in which he discussed the theme of his lecture in greater detail and talked expansively about the significance of the new African writing that was being published. This meeting was a good example of how, through experience with a primary resource person, you can be educated in greater depth and with a more memorable impact than can be obtained from reading any number of books on the subject under discussion. There is something about direct transmission from people who live, breathe, and work in a discipline to which they are devoted that comes across in a more luminous and penetrating way.

Ama Ata Aidoo was a young writer at the beginning of her career when she visited Kenya in 1970 and came to the FWC Center at Kaptagat. She had written her first play, *The Dilemma of a Ghost*, while a student at the University of Ghana, which Longman published in 1965, making her a notable voice among African women. In 1970, Longman published another of her plays, *Anowa* (based on a Ghanaian legend), and a volume of short stories, *No Sweetness Here*. By the time she arrived at the FWC Center to hold workshops and discussions with students, she was riding high on her mission to advance the image and status of women. This was truly in sync with FWC students and Aidoo held court like a force of nature. She was ebullient, challenging, humorous, and encouraging. She knew how to engage students and they were both engaged and mesmerized.

Aidoo was like the protagonists in her stories, a woman who did not accommodate to stereotypical roles. And she had a world perspective. Her brand of feminism applied across the world as far as she was concerned. She happened to be African, but women everywhere were for her the concern of her advocacy. Seven years later she published her first novel, *Our Sister Killjoy: or Reflections from a Black-Eyed Squint*. She has since published eight additional books and has had a teaching and creative writing career in Africa, Europe, and America. Interaction with a writer like Ama Ata Aidoo, who not only has a creative gift but a social mission with a world perspective, is the kind of direct encounter and experiential learning that the Friends World program was set up to foster.

•   •   •

When we landed at JFK Airport in New York on our return to the US, the cultural shock was somehow greater than when we landed at Nairobi. East Africa does that to you. Both the social ambiance and the landscape take you in and, without detection, subtly remake your perception and sense of relationship. There is an amplitude of social feeling and generosity that plays out in even casual relationships with people for which one suddenly feels nostalgic when stepping back into the American milieu. The sense of landscape with which one exists in East Africa becomes a memory of primal connection as you re-enter the dislocation and alienation of the paved over and over built environment of urban America.

The ancient and ever renewing forms of life on the African plains bring up a sense of the infinite. The way the season of the long rains renews earth's abundance verges on the miraculous. The way the sunset floods the senses and the cloud-piled evening sky slips suddenly into night leaves something of the cosmic on the edge of memory. All this, and much more, draws the mind and body into a rhythm of relationship that adds an African resonance to the rest of your life.

When we returned from East Africa, we faced a decision; we could settle back into life on Long Island, working for Friends World College at the North American Center, or we could explore a leading[13] that was moving us in another direction.

---

13   This use of the word "leading" indicates a sense guidance, of being drawn to a particular course of action. It is commonly used this way by Quakers to describe a practice of meditative discernment on what one is called, either individually or collectively, to do.

As we viewed the environmental crisis, food system security loomed large. Industrial agriculture was degrading soil health and the consumer economy was putting urban regions and even small cities and towns at the mercy of long distance food supply chains. The way in which the industrial economy was consolidating food production and elaborating its worldwide networks of distribution seemed anything but smart from the standpoint of food security.

The trajectory of this system did not match up with the requirements of resilient and sustainable community development. It matched up instead with the short-term profitability and wealth accumulation of transnational corporations and the concomitant loss of local and regional food production capacity. This loss is a setup for an environmental crisis that points directly to a societal crisis of dire consequence.

I once had a conversation with an agronomist at a conference on the future of agriculture in which he complained that "all my colleagues want talk to about is how to increase production in the next five years; I want to talk about how we will feed ourselves when we can no longer feed our combine-harvesters." Precisely! He could see the food system crisis that was coming with the end of the hydrocarbon era.

Both Ellen and I had grown up in families and communities that were highly self-provisioning with regard to local and homestead food production. We had a heritage of skills and knowledge that could be put to use in working for local food system security and sustainable community development. We were nearing our mid-thirties with two sons, Eric, 7, and Brendan, 5. We were concerned about a holistic educational environment for our sons beyond the school system. The American war in Vietnam was still raging and getting worse. I knew the hazards of returning to the resistance. I had dodged police clubs but not the tear gas at the Democratic Convention in Chicago in 1968. Students had since been shot down and killed by the Ohio National Guard on the campus of Kent State University where I had once walked to class.

We wanted to turn our collective energy in a positive direction and work for the realization of a sustainable society in a way and at a scale that could make a difference. At Friends World College we had helped develop and conduct study programs on world problems and their solutions. It was time to turn from theory to practice. We bought a farm in New Brunswick, Canada and set our compass on local food system security — local production for the local community.

Chapter Five

Vocational Interlude & A Homestead Library
Speerville, New Brunswick

If you have a garden and a library, you have everything you need.

Cicero

A room without books is like a body without a soul.

Cicero

After this bookseller's memoir has been completed, I may take up the story of North Hill Farm. If so, it will start with the sentence: "We had a farm in Canada in the hills of the Wolastoq[14] watershed." Those who have read Isak Dinesen's *Out of Africa* will recognize the echo. She begins her classic memoir with this sentence: "I had a farm in Africa at the foot of the Ngong Hills." Although I cannot expect to write about our experience of farm and community life with the limpid grace Isak Dinesen achieved in writing her book, there was an uncanny carryover for me from her experience in East Africa to my experience on our farm in New Brunswick.

Many times during our years on North Hill Farm, I would look out across the wooded valleys to the north and east as the cool,

---

14 Wolastoq is the original name of the river that flows from the forest and lake country of northern Maine, defines the border with Quebec, and then flows south through western and central New Brunswick to the Bay of Fundy. French explorer Samuel de Champlain didn't know it had a name and called it the St. John River.

early morning mist gathered and rose above the pointed firs to disappear in the growing warmth of the sun and feel something akin to the experience of Isak Dinesen. Although our forested landscape was different from that which surrounded the Ngong Hills in Kenya, a similar experience, anchored in a sense of place and nurtured by the unaccountable earth, knit both realities into one for me. Isak Dineson writes:

> ... the farm lay at an altitude of over six thousand feet. In the day-time you felt that you had got high up, near to the sun... Up in this high air you breathed easily, drawing in a vital assurance and lightness of heart. In the highlands you woke up in the morning and thought: Here I am, where I ought to be.[15]

Precisely! This was, indeed, my feeling as I gazed over the valley landscape from our hillside farm. But North Hill Farm is another story that bears telling in another way. For now, I will put on my library hat and touch lightly on the books and authors that were of special significance for me during our homestead farming years before I again became a bookseller within the academic community at the University of Pennsylvania, much to my surprise and delight.

•　•　•

In preparing for our East African sojourn, I pulled a selection of books from the shelves of my library, packed them up and posted the shipment for General Delivery to the Nairobi Post Office. I had never before left the North American continent and I wanted to keep a few books close at hand that somehow kept me grounded in the land of my birth. I knew the experience of living and working in East Africa was likely to be life altering. I was up for this step into the unknown. But my anticipation of immersion in the geography and culture of East Africa was

---

15　Isak Dinesen, *Out of Africa* (1937; rpt. New York: The Modern Library, 1952), p. 3, 4.

tempered by knowing I was rooted in a certain aspect of North American culture. At the end of our sojourn, when I shipped my travelling library back to Long Island, the books acquired in East Africa doubled its size. This combination of books was symbolic of the balancing act with which I had negotiated an intense period of cross-cultural experience.

Among the books I took with me to East Africa were some I had not yet read and some to be reread. For rereading I took a compact edition of Thoreau's *Walden*, Sarah Orne Jewett's *Country of Pointed Firs*, Gary Snyder's *Back Country*, and Kenneth Grahame's *Wind in the Willows* for reading to Eric and Brendan.

Among the books to be read, I included Snyder's just published *Earth House Hold: Technical Notes and Queries to Fellow Dharma Revolutionaries*, Stanley Diamond's *Primitive Views of the World*, Carl Ortwin Sauer's *Land and Life*, and Wendell Berry's second book of poetry, *Openings*, that I picked up in a used bookshop in Hempstead, Long Island shortly before we left for East Africa. It was a pristine, cloth-bound, 1968, first edition published by Harcourt, Brace and World. The publisher's card, indicating it had been a complimentary review copy, was tucked inside the front cover, which meant whoever they sent it to, hoping for a good review, had cashed it in at the used bookstore instead of adding it to their library.

Wendell Berry was unknown to me when I picked up this book, but I liked the feel of it and the black and white cover photograph, which looked through the author's large multi-paned window at the silhouettes of bare trees against a grey sky and low hills. I opened the book and read the first sentence on the flyleaf:

> The poems brought together in *Openings* are those of an American, a countryman, a husband and father —a man deeply concerned about the pass to which his nation has come.[16]

---

16   Wendell Berry, *Openings* (New York: Harcourt, Brace and World, 1968), flyleaf of dust jacket.

I was hooked. I opened the book, read two poems, and knew I had found a gem. I packed the book for Africa, knowing it would be a good tether to home. Like Berry, I was distressed about my nation. I was, likewise, a husband and a father, and although we were currently living on Long Island and about to leave for East Africa, I had no doubt I was "a countryman." The path to the full realization of this identity had, however, taken some unlikely turns—a university education, academic bookstore manager, college librarian, college teacher. And now, an assignment in East Africa seemed to be going even farther afield from any such identity. However, it turned out there is something about the East African landscape and its human settlements (beyond the city lights) that imprints the sense of the human-earth relationship ever more deeply into your worldview and into a more fully rounded way of seeing and feeling the intimacy with which sentient beings, including humans, are embedded in the processes of earth. All of this had the effect on me of raising the sense of being a "countryman" to the level of a global vocation.

I here use "global" in both senses: first, as a holistic awareness of an encompassing story, and second, as pertaining to the entire planetary terrain that functions as a thermodynamic, geochemical, photosynthetic, and metabolic unit, and within which all creatures, both flora and fauna of whatever magnitude, participate in a planetary process. In East Africa—the home terrain of our hominid heritage—it came to me with particular clarity that sustainable adaptation is always anchored in photosynthesis and metabolism, both of which flourish as a function of earth's soil and water environments in relation to sunlight.

The world over, this is true. Plants and animals, soil and water underwrite human adaptation. All civilizations, all human settlements, all forms of ecologically coherent adaptation to the planetary terrain are anchored in the continuing integrity of the biospheric environment. In this sense, everyone is a "countryman" even if you live in town. But some are called to the vocation. The vocational leading that came to us on our return from East Africa was homestead farming, market gardening, local food system development, and community-based economic security.

• • •

Between the time we landed back on Long Island and the establishment of North Hill Farm, we researched our options, which included living in Vermont for the fall, winter, and early spring of 1970-71. Through friends who lived in southern Vermont, we had the good fortune to be put in touch with Wolf Kahn and Emily Mason, who had a summer home on Stark Road near West Brattleboro. The property was an old hillside farm with a house and barn tucked into the slope above the open ground and backed by forest that ran to a high ridge overlooking the valley route across the Green Mountains to Bennington. We met with Wolf and Emily, struck up a good rapport, and moved in time to prepare for the coming winter. They preferred to have the house occupied year round and generously made it available to us, rent-free.

Wolf and Emily were both painters, living and working otherwise in New York City. With daughters, Cecily and Melany, they spent summers at their Vermont house. Many of Wolf Kahn's distinctive landscape paintings are associated with this place and its surrounding terrain. The large barn on the property sits on a right angle to the steep hillside with the foundation buried on the uphill side and fully exposed on the downhill side. The barn stands like a great wooden ship about to be launched. Over the years, this barn has been featured in a variety of Wolf Kahn's paintings. To call them landscape paintings is, in a way, correct, but the term does not convey the singularly unique and utterly distinct coloring, quality of light, and ambiance that characterize Wolf Kahn's paintings whether of barns, trees, or hills and valleys.

One New Year's eve, decades later, Ellen and I accompanied our son Eric and Nina Nickles (Achilles and Olga's daughter) to a party in Boston at the apartment of the woman who owned the bicycle touring company for which Nina was a tour leader. As we walked up the stairs, there on the wall of the landing was an unmistakable painting; the strokes of color, the subtle light, the barn, it was all there. It was instantly recognizable as a Wolf Kahn painting. It was worth the trip to Boston just to see this painting that brought back such good memories of our happy association with the artist and our over wintering in the Stark Road house.

When Wolf, Emily, and their daughters came to visit us in the spring 1971 before we left for New Brunswick, they presented us with a gift of fabric art from Afghanistan. We were quite touched. They had made their Vermont house available to us at no cost for seven months and now brought us a farewell gift. We had cared for and safeguarded their house for a season and they gave us a gift in return. Artists, more than most folks, tend to live in a gift economy. The fabric is too delicate to have been a rug and too small to be a bed cover. Perhaps it was used as a tablecloth. It is clearly of some age and quite worn.

The piece is a three-foot square of dusty blue, lightweight cotton into which wool yarn has been hand-stitched in dark red rectangle and triangle designs. A border of pieced fabric, cut and stitched into triangles, encloses the centre block.

Round, open islets are stitched into the whole surface of the material inside the border. Inside each islet are small round pieces of shiny metal held in place by the stitching. All this gives the piece a shimmering, diaphanous quality. One can only imagine the origin of the piece and the uses to which it was put before we received it as a gift. It now hangs on the wall of our bedroom in an area shielded from direct sunlight and reminds us of the gift of friendship, even, or perhaps especially, when contact is brief.

•   •   •

As a bookseller without a bookstore, and with my library packed up in boxes waiting for our next move, I naturally sought out bookstores wherever I had the opportunity. Fortunately, Brattleboro had a fine bookshop, tucked into the lower level of a Main Street building and aptly named, The Book Cellar. It was here I found two more Wendell Berry books, both recently published: *The Long-Legged House* and *Farming: A Hand Book*. Two books more suited to my frame of mind at the time and more aligned with the leading we were following would be hard to imagine.

The Long-Legged House is a collection of essays in which, for the first time, Wendell Berry lays out the themes that would inform the arc of his writing for the rest of his life—themes of livelihood, homestead and place-based living, local sustenance, community membership, land health, ecologically coherent adaptation, socially adept and cooperative economic relationships, and reverence, care, and nurture for the great mystery of the living world in all its forms and expressions. *Farming: A Hand Book* is the collection of poetry in which his "mad farmer" poems first appear. These poems struck a chord with readers who, like Berry, had set their hands to the work of cultural and ecological preservation but were not averse to giving McLuhan's "mechanical bride" a swift kick along the way.

From that time on I have kept track of Wendell Berry's writing and have, until recent years, collected everything he published. I still make a point to pick up the poetry, but I have fallen behind on the essay collections. Reading and pondering his poetry has helped keep me sane; writing it seems to have helped him in the same way.

Over the years, I have had the opportunity at several conferences to enjoy conversations with Wendell Berry. In addition, we have had a few rounds of correspondence, the last one as recently as August 2020. I sent him the following note and a copy of a poem:

> A friend who was life-long horse farmer in Nova Scotia died this past week. His wife sent out this poem he had recently written, which made me think of you. I understand from *Orion* magazine that your 86th birthday was also this past week. So perhaps I am serving as the conduit of a birthday gift from one horse farmer to another. Here's the poem.

                              Suddenly
          The team is fresh and stepping along,
          And the Cockshutt Giant cuts its five-foot swath.
          But progress is sure.
          Despite mares, mower, and me,
          The stand withstands, and the day grows short.
          Suddenly, the end's in sight.
          And then—it happens every time—
          The stand falls with surprising speed.
          It is finished.
          Like the early rounds of a halyard
          The seasons of youth were long.
          Now time hastens.
          But still I cannot see the end.
          When I do,
          How can I fail to be astonished at how quickly
          It is finished?

Wendell Berry wrote back;

> Ed Belzer's lovely poem touches me deeply, as you
> knew it would. I thank you for the poem and for your
> thoughtfulness in sending it to me.

                    •   •   •

In taking up an agricultural vocation, we naturally added a
number of books on farming, gardening, and the care of farm
animals to our library. Since Ellen and I had grown up with the
basics, we didn't need introductory instruction. Aside from Rodale's *Encyclopaedia of Organic Gardening*, which is a great reference
book, especially for trouble-shooting, we picked up books that
helped hone our management skills with regard to animal health.
We had grown up with cows and chickens, but a flock of sheep
and a small dairy goat operation were new to us. We lost our
first dairy goat to ketosis after she freshened. We researched that
problem and never lost another one.

Beyond guides and manuals, I continued to research the history of agriculture in the scope of human settlements and the development of civilization. I had read Carl Ortwin Sauer's seminal geographical essays collected in *Land and Life* (1963). In addition, a collection of his studies with the title *Seed, Spades, Hearths & Herds: The Domestication of Animals and Foodstuffs*, which had been published in 1952 by the American Geographical Society, was reissued in 1974 by The MIT Press. This was a prize addition to my research into Sauer's work. And then, in 1981, Turtle Island Foundation brought out *Selected Essays 1963-1975 Carl Sauer*, a splendid collection of his research reports and presentations that had not yet been gathered into a book. I now had a rich trove of Sauer material to study and ponder.

Carl Sauer was an ecological thinker before the significance of this worldview was recognized. His command of cultural, geomorphic, and biotic data, through which the sequences, phases, and adaptations of the human-earth relationship can be traced, is particularly comprehensive, and the narrative skill with which he describes his findings and understandings engages the mind *and* the imagination. All this is well and beautifully illustrated in the geography textbook he composed for middle school students published by Rand McNally in 1939 — *Man in Nature: America Before the Days of the White Man; A First Book in Geography*. The book had not previously come to my attention and I was astonished when I found a copy in a used bookstore in Houlton, Maine.

Man in Nature is a classic textbook from another era. Its 8 ½ x 10 ½ trim size is bound in a rugged cloth cover. When you open the book, a typographically arresting title page is faced by a full page, full colour illustration of "Tropical Indian Farmers." The table of contents announces the journey of human and environmental geography on which the book will take its readers. Virtually every page thereafter includes strikingly detailed, black and white illustrations of the stories and descriptions that unfold on page after page of text. The book covers every environmental zone and human adaptation from the Isthmus of Panama and the Caribbean Islands to the Bering Sea and Greenland.

My brother and I grew up on the watershed divide of the Chagrin and Cuyahoga Rivers in northeast Ohio. We were aware of the Indigenous people—the Erie, Seneca, Wyandot, and Shawnee—that had been at home in this region before the invasion of colonial frontiersmen and the US Army had pushed them out. We roamed the woods in their shadow, built huts and lean-tos for camping out and walked the ploughed fields looking for arrowheads. If Carl Sauer's magnificent book, *Man in Nature*, had come to our attention in those days, we would have studied it like a bible.

In 1864, Vermont political and civic leader, polymath, and international diplomat George Perkins Marsh published *Man and Nature: Or, Physical Geography as Modified by Human Action* in which he describes the repeated and alarming instances throughout history of environmental degradation resulting from human exploitation. When Marsh surveyed this ecological wreckage, he viewed the human species as a force standing alongside Nature but failing in good management. His book triggered the beginning of the American conservation and resource management movement. Carl Sauer, of course, was thoroughly familiar with Marsh's landmark study, to the point of wanting to call a 1955 Werner-Gren Foundation conference, which he helped organize, the "Marsh Festival." It came to be called "Man's Role in Changing the Face of the Earth."[17]

The title of Sauer's 1939 middle school textbook echoes the title of Marsh's 1864 book, but with a significant difference. Marsh's book is called *Man and Nature*, Sauer's book is called *Man*

---

17 The proceedings of this extraordinary conference were published under this title in 1956 by the University of Chicago Press in a 1236 page book of extraordinary significance for the development of a culturally and scientifically integrated ecological worldview. Seventy-seven researchers and scholars from a multiplicity of fields converged on the theme for a full week. The list of participants is a who's who of foundational ecological thinkers on whose shoulders we now stand. Carl Sauer, Lewis Mumford, and Marston Bates were the conference organizers.

in Nature. The change from *and* to *in* makes all the difference; it signals the change from an anthropocentric to a biocentric or ecocentric worldview. But the change, even now at this late date, is incomplete; human aggrandizement dies hard and is still, in 2025, hanging on with an absurd tenacity. But the work of Carl Sauer and his colleagues during this time mapped the human-earth relationship in such a way that the ecological worldview could get a footing in the culture. We are, however, still in a battle to make the guidance of this great accomplishment fully manifest.

In 1938, Sauer gave a presidential address titled "Theme of Plant and Animal Destruction in Economic History" to the Eighth Social Science Research Conference. After describing the destruction of vegetative habitats stretching from Cape Verde to Mongolia by domestic animal overgrazing, and the similar loss of productive lands around the Mediterranean basin for the same reason, he writes as follows:

> With these two major exceptions, we know of scarcely any record of destructive exploitation in all the span of human existence until we enter the period of modern history, when transatlantic expansion of European commerce, peoples, and government take place. Then begins what may well be the tragic rather than the great age of man. ...
>
> In the late eighteenth century the progressively and rapidly cumulative destructive effects of European exploitation become marked. They are indeed an important and integral part of the industrial and commercial revolution. In the space of a century and a half—only two full lifetimes—more damage has been done to the productive capacity of the world than in all of human history preceding.

Sauer goes on to detail three zones of extreme destruction that are a setup for habitat deterioration and socioeconomic catastrophe for human settlements: 1) biodiversity loss of animal species, 2) biodiversity loss of plant species, especially the genetic narrowing of food plants, and 3) soil fertility loss from mono-cropping and soil loss from erosion, which is like the nail in the coffin for productive land use and sustainable human settlement. He comments further:

> These losses are in many cases irreparable. ... We cannot assume, as we are prone to do, an indefinite elastic power of mind over matter. ...
>
> Our ideology is that of an indefinitely expanding universe, for we are the children of frontiersman. We are prone to think of an ever ample world created for our benefit, by optimistic anthropocentric habits of thinking. ... This "frontier" attitude has the recklessness of an optimism that has become habitual, but which is a residual from the brave days when north-European freebooters overran the world and put it under tribute. We have not yet learned the difference between yield and loot. We do not like to be economic realists.[18]

• • •

We had come to farming with a critique of the fragility and ecological incoherence of the industrial, globalized food system well in mind. We had taken over a farm property that had upland fields and hillside pasture, along with a six-acre apple orchard, all laid out on terrain that had once been forestland and had been cleared and settled in the early 1800s. The relatively thin layer of topsoil that had been built up since the last glaciation was strewn with sizable rocks and underlain in many places with ledge. The soil that had accumulated over all those centuries was perfect for sustaining a vast, continually self-renewing forest region. It was not great for farming.

---

18 *Journal of Farm Economics*, Volume 20:4 (November 1938), p. 765-775.

The numerous rock piles that dotted the fields were an indication of the work our predecessors had undertaken to convert rocky forestland to usable farmland. To a certain extent we were bound to continue this rock pile business depending on the kind of farming enterprise we developed. This was marginal farmland. There was much to ponder. It wasn't at all clear this land should have been cleared of its tree cover in the first place, but here we were, choosing to pick up a heritage and intent on carrying it into the future.

At one period in its history New Brunswick had more sheep than people and for good reason; sheep are well suited for keeping on marginal farmland. Sheep made a good contribution to the economies of the traditional, small scale, mixed farm operations that were established as European colonists and Loyalist refugees from the American Rebellion became settlers in this region of Maritime Canada. For a variety of reasons, however, sheep farming had diminished in the province since the end of World War Two, but it made good sense for our farm and we "went into sheep," as the expression has it. Our main farming goal was to develop a market garden business and we wanted a good supply of animal manure to fertilize our gardens. Sheep manure is one of the best for building up well-balanced, sustainable, organic soil fertility. Our hilltop soil was thin but it was a good clay/loam mixture that responded well to the application of sheep manure, pulverized limestone (to counteract its acidity), and cover cropping. Our small livestock and market garden farm took shape and became our family's livelihood base for a variety of other community development activities, among which was the establishment of a farm market cooperative in the town of Woodstock, which in 2023 celebrated its 50th anniversary.

When you take your bearings for a land-based way of life, the primary question shifts from "who are we" to "where are we." We were now the proprietors of a farm carved out of the forest with fields that, if not regularly mowed for hay and regularly grazed by livestock, would quickly begin to grow poplar and birch, followed by spruce, maple, ash, fir, cedar, and pine.

In some cases, this was fine by us. Some fields were even less than marginal, with rock piles so frequent and hay crop so thin it made no sense to work at enhancing their fertility. We happily watched these sub-marginal fields return to forestland while we built up the fertility of more favourably situated and more easily maintained ground.

While I was improving my grasp of where we were and the requirements of ecologically coherent farming on this place, I continued my book-guided study of the landscapes of earth, the panorama of human settlements, the various strategies of adaptation, and the variety of cultural stories humans have developed to make sense of where they are and what they are doing. Some of the books that lent wings to my research came with me to North Hill Farm unread and now commanded my attention. Many others were acquired during those farming years and joined the homestead library that surrounded me with the same effect of accompaniment as the bookstores of my past and the library at Friends World College.

Among the books I had long intended to read was *Eyes of Discovery: America as Seen By the First Explorers* by John Bakeless. My Iowa City bookstore colleague and friend, Gerald Stevenson, had enthusiastically urged it on me as a book I must read. I eventually picked up the 1961 Dover paperback edition of this 1950 J. B. Lippincott book. Dover paperbacks were notable for their sewn bindings, which made them exceptionally durable. This was fortuitous since this book traveled with me to East Africa and back as a kind of talisman, but without being read. I often have a sense of timing for reading a particular book. It's a bit uncanny, but it happens often enough that despite my overt intentions I have learned to be guided in this respect. Now that we were settled in the northeast corner of the continent for the foreseeable future, and in a landscape that had retained much of its heritage, the time for reading *Eyes of Discovery* had arrived.

Continentally speaking, this splendid assembly of narratives provides a unique perspective on where we are as non-Indigenous settlers. Working from first person accounts of what was seen and encountered before the inroads and depravations of colonial settlement altered the landscape and habitat, Bakeless offers a fully rounded view of what seemed a "wilderness" to Europeans but was a home place of identity and abundance for the communities of Indigenous people who inhabited what came to be called North America. For a window on this perspective, Wendell Berry offers the following instructive reflection:

> It is thought that the beech forests of the Midwest, in the time before the white invasion, produced an annual nut crop of a billion bushels. Suppose that early in our history we had learned, like the Indians, to make use of this bounty, and of the rest of the natural produce of the country. We would have been unimaginably different, and would have been less in need of forgiveness. Instead of asking what was already here that might be of use to us, we hastened to impose on the face of the new country, like the scraps and patches of a collage, the fields and crop rows and fences of Europe. We destroyed the abundance that lay before us simply by being unwilling or unable to acknowledge that it was there. We did not know where we were, and to avoid the humility and labor of our ignorance, we pretended to be where we had come from. And so there is a sense in which we are still not here. Because we have ignored the place we have come to, our presence here remains curiously accidental, as though we came by misapprehension or mistake, like birds driven out to sea by a storm.[19]

Wendell Berry's reflection set me to researching food environments, food systems, and food security at a deeper level. My interest had been focused primarily on contemporary food

---

19   Wendell Berry, *The Long-Legged House* (1969; rpt. New York: Ballantine Books, 1971), p. 205-206.

systems and on food security for the future. Our food system heritage was in small-scale farming and gardening. With the acquisition of a farm in New Brunswick, we had now staked out a vocational return to this heritage.

With this combination of heritage, vocational path, and research interests in mind, I lined up a number of books on the "to be read" shelf of my library: *The Care of the Earth: A History of Husbandry* (1962) by Russell Lord; *Plough and Pasture: The Early History of Farming* (1953, 1961) by E. Cecil Curwen and Gudmund Hatt; *Soil and Civilization* (1952, 1976) by Edward Hyams; *An Agricultural Testament* (1943) by Sir Albert Howard; and *Plants, Man & Life* (1952, 1967) by Edgar Anderson, and *Farmers of Forty Centuries: Permanent Agriculture in China, Korea, and Japan* (1911) by F. H. King. I had seen repeated references to this latter book over the course of my studies and eventually tracked down a copy of a 1949 edition republished by Rodale Press. I spent many hours with these volumes over a couple of years, often late at night with the wood-burning stove cranked up and a wind-blown snowstorm whipping around the house and barns.[20] It took me the better part of two years to make my way through these six books, partly because they weren't the only books I was reading, partly because I savoured this grand tour through the origins, history, and practices of agriculture, and partly because I was beginning to write for publication on my experience as a market gardener and homestead farmer.

The Care of the Earth is a literary treasure. Russell Lord (1895-1964) grew up on what would now be called a "hobby farm." His father was an investment banker in Baltimore who moved his family to a small farm in the Maryland countryside when Russell was thirteen. They were an early part of the "back to the land" movement, which is a perpetual motif of 20th century North

---

20 I was often up past midnight on the late winter birth-watch when lambing started and we had to check frequently during the night on the ewes that had not eaten at the evening feeding—a sure sign they would lamb during the night and need moving to a closed pen with a heat-lamp.

American life. Russell Lord took to agriculture in his own way and according to his particular talents; he became, among other things, an agricultural journalist. *The Care of Earth* is his last book and he poured his vast knowledge and his love of the subject into it. But what makes it so enjoyable is the grace and eloquence of his literary style. It's the kind of book that even if you're not especially interested in the history of husbandry is hard to put down once you start reading. His enthusiasm is infectious and the enjoyable lilt of his somewhat old school phrasing pulls you on, page after page. Lord was so imbued with a sense of earth's interdependent processes that his narrative has a truly ecological cast. Biographer Margaret Eppig[21] identifies him as a thinker and writer who is the bridge between conservation agriculture and the development of a fully rounded ecological worldview.

During this time, I also had Dee Brown's new book on my reading list—*Bury My Heart at Wounded Knee: An Indian History of the American West* (1971). The first time I tried to read it, I stopped on page 27. Here concludes the story of how in 1864 Kit Carson, commanding a regiment of the US Army, defeated the Navaho people at Canyon de Chelly. It was a prolonged, scorched earth campaign that finally brought the last of the starving families out of hiding into captivity. And then, to prevent any resettlement, Carson ordered the destruction of all remaining Navaho properties in the Canyon "including their beloved peach orchards, more than five thousand trees." I could read no further. I closed the book and didn't return to it for some months. I kept thinking of the number of peach trees as well as their destruction and added this notation to my research; "Five thousand peach trees! That's real agriculture, real horticulture."

Plough and Pasture opened my eyes still further to the extent that certain Indigenous peoples of the continent were substantial agriculturists. In this case, we have the marauding and genocidal activities of the American Continental Army

---

21   Margaret Eppig, 2017. *Russell Lord and the Permanent Agriculture Movement: An Environmental Biography.* Antioch University of New England, PhD dissertation, 2017.

to thank for documenting this information. On May 31, 1779, George Washington explicitly abandoned the traditional European practice of limited warfare and sent General John Sullivan his marching orders against the Iroquois that included the following instructions:

> The Expedition you are appointed to command is to be directed against the hostile tribes of the Six Nations of Indians, ... The immediate objects are the total destruction and devastation of their settlements ... It will be essential to ruin their crops now in the ground and prevent their planting more. ... [P]arties should be detached to lay waste all the settlements around, with instructions to do it in the most effectual manner, that the country may not be merely overrun, but destroyed. But you will not by any means listen to any overture of peace before the total ruinment of their settlements is effected. ... [22]

The assault lasted from June through September of 1779. The Iroquois fled north into hiding but with winter coming and their food supplies destroyed many succumbed to starvation. Some made it to the safety of Canada where they sheltered with the British Army. General Sullivan reported the complete burning of forty Iroquois villages, including one hundred and sixty thousand bushels of stored corn. He documented the complete destruction of extensive, newly planted cornfields, including one at Chemung of some sixty acres.

Plough and Pasture also reports that at the time of early contact with Europeans, the Hurons at Lake Simcoe in southern Ontario had stores of corn adequate for three years, and that each of several tribes along the upper Missouri River Valley had in the range of a thousand acres planted in corn. Each family often had two or

---

22   Curwen, E. Cecil and Gudmund Hatt, 1953, 1961 *Plough and Pasture: The Early History of Farming.* https://founders.archives.gov/documents/Washington/03-20-02-0661. Lines 1-5, 25-27, 60-61.

three acres under cultivation. Some especially industrious families were known to have seven or eight acres in crops. Along the lower Mississippi, the Natchez were virtually full-time farmers, deriving most of their living from agriculture. To the east, among the Muskhogean and Yuchi peoples, even adult males worked the fields, a thing unheard of in most other tribes. In addition to the main crop of corn (maize), squash, pumpkins, beans, gourds, melons, sunflowers and tobacco were widely cultivated. Over eleven hundred wild plant species were also utilized for food and medicines. It is true that in some areas of the continent tribal communities relied heavily on hunting and fishing for food supplies. But in areas where crops could be grown, Indigenous agriculture was often equal to and sometimes exceeded that of Celtic and Anglo-Saxon farmers in Europe who were using oxen and ploughs. Even the European settlers of the Ohio Valley, who used horses and ploughs, rarely cultivated more land per family than the Indigenous communities of the upper Missouri.

Clearly, these examples of sustainable food systems indicate a collective knowledge within communities of people who knew *where they were, how the world around them worked, and what they were doing in relation to their environment.* The history of destruction that descended on them is heartbreaking, but at least we know, with respect to their sustainable food systems, that a mutually enhancing human-earth relationship can be achieved. This relationship will look different in different eras and under different circumstances, but it is not a fantasy; it is a requirement of ecologically coherent adaptation.

Harper & Row promoted their 1976 paperback edition of *Soil and Civilization* with the following statement; "The first book of its kind to cover the vast panorama of human history from a strictly ecological point of view." This may be an exaggeration since Lewis Mumford had been writing and publishing books with an ecological point of view since the 1930s, but it is true that *Soil and Civilization* is unique in its focus on the types, conditions, use, and misuse of the earth's topsoil across all cultural regions. It's also uniquely disturbing; agriculture and animal husbandry, when thoughtlessly concentrated on wealth accumulation and exploited to feed burgeoning urban populations, has repeatedly destroyed the fertility of soils and triggered its loss to erosion — both one-way tickets to cultural regression and adaptational collapse.

One bright note in his survey and analysis is that in northern Europe, where small-scale, mixed crop, and livestock farming has continued for centuries, the fertility of agricultural soils has been maintained and even improved. The regular application of animal manures is the key. This is the heritage of small-scale agriculture and traditional knowledge. I was glad to find this nugget of confirmation for the kind of operation we were running on North Hill Farm. It made me more willing to put my midnight energy into another walk to the barn through blowing snow to see if another lamb had been born since I last checked. It wasn't just lambs the ewes were producing. After a long winter we would have tons of sheep manure with which to enrich our market gardens as well.

Farmers of Forty Centuries is one of the most astounding and confounding books on farming a modern agriculturist will ever read. The book is truly in a class by itself. I can do no better than to quote from the cover flap of the Rodale edition.

> Dr. King, a former chief of the Division of Soil Management of the US Department of Agriculture, went to the Orient in the early 1900s as an agricultural visitor. He traveled through Japan, Korea, and China, photographing the fields, talking to farmers, and everywhere noting the exact methods used. He wanted to find out how people could farm the same fields for 4000 years without destroying their fertility. He especially wanted to see how Oriental farmers could support families of 12 to 15 people on less than two acres, and do it generation after generation ...

> What Dr. King saw was a farm system where nothing was wasted. Fields were carefully terraced so there

was little erosion. Silt that was carried into canals by heavy rains was scooped up and put back on the fields. All plant, animal, and human wastes were put back on the land, usually after being composted. Farmers worked on such wastes for one, three, or even six months, said Dr. King, "in order to bring them to the most efficient form to serve as manure for the soil, or as feed for the crop."

Human wastes were almost the lifeblood of Oriental agriculture, Dr. King found. Farmers made attractive screens near their fields so passersby would honor them by leaving behind some human fertilizer. All families saved their toilet wastes and sold them to farmers. Cities found their human wastes to be a net profit instead of a liability as in the United States. In 1908, Shanghai sold one Chinese contractor 78,000 tons of human wastes for $31,000 in gold! ...

Dr. King details information on composting, inter-tillage, crop rotation, irrigation, and green manuring, and sprinkles it with lore about the peoples and their culture.[23]

Farmers of Forty Centuries is 431 pages long with 248 photographs. It is a virtual manual on the organic management of soil fertility in perpetuity. It is an inspiring confirmation that human civilizations can achieve and maintain a mutually enhancing human-earth relationship. A number of print-on-demand publishers have recently added *Farmers of Forty Centuries* to the books they have digitized and can now supply to those who seek a copy for their library. *An Agricultural Testament* (1943) is Sir Albert Howard's classic contribution to understanding organic

---

23   F. H. King, *Farmers of Forty Centuries: Permanent Agriculture in China, Korea, and Japan* (1911; rpt. Emmaus PA: Rodale Press [n.d.]).

soil fertility and how to maintain it in conditions of intensive cultivation. From his decades of research and experimentation in Britain and India, his book, like Dr. King's, is a report and a manual. Howard's book, however, is science based rather than anecdotal and is furnished with detailed instructions on methods and practices of composting. As often happens in scientific research oriented toward sustainable cultivation, practices that have endured in the folk wisdom of peasant agriculture prove to be of high merit. The science of composting is a good example, which Howard presents in great detail and on which he comes to this conclusion:

> ... attempts have been made to prepare humus [compost] without animal wastes. The results have not fulfilled expectations. ... The organisms which synthesize humus are not properly fed. ... No one has yet succeeded in establishing an efficient and permanent system of agriculture without livestock.[24]

A largely vegetarian diet is, in some ways, a good thing from both an ethical and an environmental point of view. But if the exercise of that diet depends on ingredients produced, processed, and transported by the fossil-fuel-powered industrial food system, the ethical and environmental considerations change; with contemporary biodiversity loss and the climate change effect, they change dramatically. Produce from local farms that raise livestock and manure their soil may be a better choice for both ethical and environmental reasons. Under the present circumstances, a few meat products from local organic farms may actually be an ethical upgrade in dietary choice over a strict vegetarian diet. As Michael Pollan, author of *Omnivores' Dilemma*, advises, "Eat food, mostly vegetables, not too much." (For Michael Pollan, "Eat food" means *real* food, as distinguished from, as he puts it, "food like substances.")

---

24 Albert Howard, *An Agricultural Testament* (New York: Oxford University Press, 1943), p. 65.

Plants, Man and Life (1952, 1967) by Edgar Anderson is the literary *crème de la crème* of this collection. Although Anderson's scholarly papers on the subject preceded this book, and a variety of books that treat the theme have since followed, *Plants, Man and Life* will never lose its attraction as a reader's delight. Here is an insight as to why this is the case. In the Preface to the 1967 edition, the author writes:

> When I started to write this book in the 1940s, I was given the good advice: "Don't write for an imaginary public. Think of some actual person as your reader; write the book for him." Ever since my late teens I had been explaining botany to visitors at various botanical gardens. Those I most enjoyed had deep-seated curiosity; good, disciplined minds; broad interests; but little technical understanding of plants. ... It was years after the book appeared before I knew it really appealed to such readers. ...

> It was not, however, the book my publishers set out to get. They had accurately detected a ground swell of interest in the story of the plants by which man lives; an interesting digest of what botany knows about the subject should have a ready sale. I presented them instead with a detailed exposition of what even the authorities did not know. ... Important technical information of new kinds was piling up rapidly, but no one was scanning the whole wide field to see how everything might fit together.

> At first the editors tried to keep me on track; ... Fortunately for my book, the firm went through a violent crisis having nothing to do with me personally. ... Eventually they were most cooperative in publishing *Plants, Man and Life*, the obverse of the book they originally planned ...

> All this was 15 years ago. Enough botanists, eco-
> logists, geographers, geneticists, and anthropologists
> who read the book as young men want their students
> to read it today, which justifies a new edition.[25]

This explains why *Plants, Man and Life* is a book not to be missed by anyone who is concerned to understand the fundamentals of the human-earth relationship. Edgar Anderson's effort to scan "the whole wide field to see how everything might fit together" produced a book that, like Aldo Leopold's *Sand County Almanac* and Carl Sauer's *Land and Life,* stands at the door through which an increasing range of people from earth system scientists to homestead farmers have now walked into the full consciousness of the ecological worldview.

Decades later, after we had retired from farming and I was happily back in the bookstore business, another wide scope book on food system adaptation was published that I immediately added to my library—*A History of World Agriculture: From the Neolithic Age to the Current Crisis* (2006) by French scholars, Marcel Mazoyer and Laurene Roudart. At five hundred and twenty-eight pages, it is truly a Lewis Mumford kind of book; the kind of book that gets written only when authors dedicate their research and narrative skill to telling a world and history encompassing story from the point of view of the common good. Mazoyer (an agricultural historian) and Roudart (an agricultural engineer) are engaged scholars who not only present the results of their research but also energetically weigh in against the so-called "modernization" of agriculture that captures and encloses resources, destroys traditional farming, impoverishes its family and community practitioners, and is bent on increasing wealth for the already stunningly rich financial elite of the world. Quoting from the publisher's statement,

---

25   Edgar Anderson, *Plants, Man and Life.*(1952; rpt. Berkeley, CA: University of Californian Press, 1967), p vii-ix. The use of male pronouns throughout is, of course, a sign of the cultural times. The author was born in 1897.

"[They] show how agricultural techniques developed in different regions of the world, and how this extraordinary wealth of knowledge, tradition, and natural variety is endangered today by global capitalism, as it forces the agrarian heritages of the world to conform to the norms of profit. ... Mazoyer and Roudart propose an alternative global strategy that can safeguard the economies of the poor countries, reinvigorate the global economy, and create a liveable future for all.[26]

A powerful and moving literary analog can be found in John Berger's magnificent trilogy, *Into their Labours*, the individual volumes of which are *Pig Earth* (1979), *Once in Europa* (1987), and *Lilac and Flag* (1990). (The trilogy title is taken from the Gospel of John 4:38. "Others have laboured and ye are entered into their labours.") The linked stories start with a fully intact European peasant community in a mountain and valley region, and then chronicle the economic, social, and psychic disruption visited on the inhabitants by the increasingly penetrating incursions of capital-driven "modernization." The stories follow the family descendants into the disorientation of the contemporary world, and then into the harsh and socially diminished regression of a dystopian future. Despite the dispiriting trajectory of the saga, the author's love for his characters, and his portrayal of their tenacity and ingenuity in coping with their circumstances, makes this work one to live with in memory and in periodic rereading. After I picked up *Lilac and Flag*—the final volume—at my hometown bookstore, I opened it while waiting at the Main Street crosswalk and read:

> The hay
> smelt of how
> the sky loved the earth

---

26   Marcel Mazoyer and Laurence Roudart, *A History of World Agriculture: From the Neolithic Age to the Current Crisis*. (New York: Monthly Review Press, 2006), back cover publisher's statement.

This was perfect. I knew from experience exactly what this expressed. And I was sure I would be reading *Into their Labours* to the end of my days.

And, finally, to wind up this part of my discourse, I discovered years later, when no longer farming and in transition from frontline bookselling to publishing, that Louisiana State University Press had recently published *Carl Sauer on Culture and Land: Readings and Commentaries* (2009) edited by William M. Denevan and Kent Mathewson. With this gathering of previous uncollected studies, transcripts of presentations, including informal remarks, along with commentaries and section introductions by other scholars, another major selection of Sauer's enduring work is now in print. It's a four hundred and fifty-eight page book. I've barely made a dent in it but it stays on my reading table. It will probably "do me out," as we say in these parts after a certain age when we accomplish a solid piece of barn or house repair. But even if I don't read the whole of its contents, it's a special pleasure to have a book with Carl Ortwin Sauer's photo on the cover. The visage is rugged, the eyes are smiling, and that ubiquitous pipe is clamped firmly in his teeth—a nostalgic reminder of the old days when such manly accouterments were *de rigueur*.

•   •   •

The last three decades of the 20th century were the years during which the ecological worldview passed from being the outlook of biologists, natural history scholars, and a growing cadre of earth system scientists into the mainstream awareness of educated and reasonably curious citizens. As a cultural phenomenon, I think it's fair to say a tipping point was reached. This is not to say the obscurantist mindset that sees earth as merely a repository of raw materials for exploitation gave up calling the shots. But it is to observe that the logic of the ecological worldview is compelling in a way that guarantees its ascendancy. The subterfuge and dishonesty with which, for example, fossil fuel corporations pushed back against the science of climate change and global warming is sad evidence of what it's like to be on the losing end of a major cultural shift. Knowing what we now know may not spare our civilization a severe wrenching since it appears corrective efforts are coming too late. But there is now an unstoppable realization that earth's planetary systems bat last and always bat 1,000.[27]

This was a time when an increasing number and variety of ecologically oriented books came to be published. They ranged from reports on the work of earth system scientists and conservation biologists to the analysis of culture and natural history narratives. At first, being a book collector, a student of social ecology, and an ecologically oriented farmer, I systematically acquired these books as they appeared. But then, as the numbers mounted, budget limitations and common sense kicked in. There's a current joke in which one farmer asks another what he would do if he won the lottery. "I guess I'd keep farmin' 'till it was gone," comes the answer. North Hill Farm was never in that money-losing situation, but thrift was necessarily our watchword and I had to be increasingly selective in expanding my library. My rule became, a book purchased was a book read. No more collecting because the book added nicely to the scope of my library. A limited budget and limited time for reading kept my collecting impulse reigned in.

●　　　●　　　●

Among the authors whose books were integral to the ecology section of my library, and which I studied closely during our farming years, are James Lovelock, Thomas Berry, Barry Commoner, and Aldo Leopold. The work of these four in particular was central

---

27　A baseball metaphor from the seasonal batting averages of players. A player who never fails to make a hit when they come to bat would have a perfect batting average, i.e., 1,000. The metaphor is sometimes phrased as, "Mother Nature bats last, and she always bats 1,000." Picture it like this; Mother Nature always comes to bat in the bottom of the ninth inning and never fails to make the hit that determines the outcome of the game. The geophysics, biochemistry, and atmospheric dynamics of the planet control the tipping points of human adaptation for good or ill, and there is no way around this ecological reality. Earth systems bat last. Human civilizations adapt—or else.

to the way I developed a profile of the ecological worldview. This outline of understanding became especially useful in preparing presentations and in guiding the writing I was doing. I came to think of these scholars and writers as representing four tracks of guidance and a review of their significance is a fitting way to wind up this section of my cultural memoir.

In the scientific track we have James Lovelock with "The Gaia Hypothesis." In the cultural track we have Thomas Berry with "The New Story." In the ecology and economic adaptation track we have Barry Commoner with "The Closing Circle." In the human-earth relationship track we have Aldo Leopold with "The Land Ethic."

In considering James Lovelock's work, a clear distinction must be made between his formulation of the Gaia hypothesis and the subsequent adoption and promotion of the concept by others. The scientific work and scientific reasoning so ably recounted and illustrated in his book, *Gaia: A New Look at Life on Earth* (1979), has stood the test of more than four decades. Through his experimental work on the interaction of chemical elements and compounds in earth history and in the development of life, James Lovelock recognized a feedback and regulatory process. The history of this process helps provide an explanatory context for the persistence and flourishing of life within the environments of the planet. The evidence with which he was working led to a surprising and compelling conclusion; the evolution of the chemical composition of the atmosphere, and its increasing suitability for the flourishing of biotic processes, could only be explained, in scientific terms, through the regulatory contribution of the whole biotic complex itself—the biosphere. The evidence indicated that once having gotten started, life, as a collective phenomenon, became a direct contributing agent to the maintenance of earth's atmosphere within a certain range of chemical composition—the very range, it turned out, required for the further development of life. And it is only through this continuing regulation of the atmosphere by planetary life that planetary life continues to exist and is able to flourish with a high level of diversity.

The Gaia hypothesis provides ecological intuition with a comprehensive scientific context. People who were predisposed toward seeing Earth as a holistic process, responded with delight. Some elders from within Indigenous cultural traditions responded with bemusement and a kind of patient tolerance. They said, in effect; "That's good medicine you have there. Too bad it took you so long to come up with it. Welcome to the Circle of Creation." Certain people, who had always regarded Earth's environment as a stockpile of raw materials for human manipulation and consumption, became alarmed that their industrial ventures and the quest for endless economic growth and wealth accumulation could now be held to account against the history and science of biotic integrity. Lovelock's scientific work provides a comprehensive context for the study of ecological relationships. It sets all life communities, including the human, squarely within the history of earth process, and shows them to be entirely beholden for survival to the continuing integrity of Gaia—life process at the planetary level.

Thomas Berry, a Catholic priest, trained in theology and the history of culture, came to regard himself as a "geologian." After a long life in the scholarship of religion and culture, Berry developed an understanding of the human story that brings the human-earth relationship into focus. He sees the human-earth relationship as central to the unfolding of culture, and all the facets of guidance, adaptation, and behaviour that culture encompasses. He observes that modern Western cultures are in a state of confusion with regard to guidance and adaptation, and are destructively floundering with regard to the human-earth relationship. The story of human origin, cultural development, and moral orientation that has been built up out of the Judaic-Christian-Islamic complex and filtered through the Greco-Roman heritage has become seriously dysfunctional. Individuals and subculture groups may still organize their lives and behaviour according to some version of this "old story," but in its larger public and cultural dimensions it is failing to provide adequate guidance.

Among the most notable examples of this failure is the contemporary state of the human-earth relationship. Berry notes this cultural failure as an autistic-like blindsiding of the organic circumstances of our lives and of earth's biotic processes in general. The Western narrative has not engaged the human-earth relationship in a way that offers adequate guidance. Instead, it has spawned a dominion story that now provides the only comprehensive guidance taken seriously at a public level in modern societies. This is the narrative of technological domination, maximum resource exploitation, unfettered capital accumulation, and unlimited economic growth. This story is promoted, and largely accepted, as the only reasonable scenario for the human-earth relationship.

Thomas Berry describes an alternative. He sees a "new story" and a new sense of guidance in a composite narrative of scientific cosmology, evolutionary biology, global cultural history, and ecological knowledge. He combines the story of earth as it has emerged from cosmic process, the story of life as it has emerged from earth process, and the story of the human as it has emerged within earth's biosphere. He sees ecological understanding emerging from both scientific work and an increased awareness of the beauty and diversity of earth's features and inhabitants. He introduces this "new story" in his book, *The Dream of Earth* (1988). In *The Universe Story* (1992) — written with mathematical cosmologist Brian Swimme — he presents the whole sweep of cosmic unfolding, earth history, and human emergence. In *The Great Work: Our Way Into the Future* (1999) he details how the new guidance we need emerges from ecological understanding and leads to the only environmental stance that makes sense for a society, a culture, a civilization — indeed, for the whole human enterprise — if it hopes to endure and flourish; he identifies that stance as "a mutually enhancing human-earth relationship."

The concept of a "mutually enhancing human-earth relationship" is one of Tom Berry's ecological guidance masterstrokes. It is a transforming conceptual advance over the conventional dualism that sees humans on one side and "Nature" on the other.

As Berry reminds us, the context is always the biosphere and biospheric relationships. The human-earth relationship is our primary reality. "Mutually enhancing human-earth relationship" expresses precisely the dynamic to which ecologically sound adaptation aspires.

Berry is also responsible for introducing the concept "earth-process" into contemporary discourse. This is a functionally helpful replacement for the concept of "Nature," which is made up of a confusing array of quasi-theological cultural constructions. Earth-process, the actual geophysical terrain of the planet and the biotic flourishing in all its diverse complexity, is what we are dealing with, not some metaphysical unity called "Nature." Which is not to say earth-process does not have a "program." As James Lovelock has shown, it certainly does. A mutually enhancing human-earth relationship is about living in sync with earth-process. Berry's clarifying concepts have been of cardinal importance in the development of the ecological worldview.

While Lovelock speaks to the scientific track, Berry incorporates the scientific perspective into the story of culture and re-presents the human as a constituent part of earth's emergence and un-folding. Berry's work honours the scientific dimension and the cultural dimension in a fully rounded "new story." This new story is a primary opening to the ecological worldview.

Less than a decade after Canadian entomologist Brian Hocking published his wake-up-call book, *Biology or Oblivion: Lessons from the Ultimate Science* (1965), Barry Commoner, also a biologist, published a book that picked up on Hocking's theme and raised the alarm to such a degree, and with such authority, that it received major media attention. *The Closing Circle: Nature, Man, and Technology* (1971) was published by Knopf, received major review attention, and became a prime text of the emerging environmental movement. As a professional researcher and educator on the physiochemical basis of biological processes, Commoner is especially qualified to address the fundamental conflict between biospheric integrity and the technology of our economic system. He points out that behind the form and functioning of earth's biotic environment there is, so to speak, two to three billion years of "research and development."

As a way of understanding the intervention of modern technology into this context, he offers a striking analogy. If you open the back of a fine Swiss watch and poke a sharp pencil into its works, there is an infinitesimal chance you will improve the functioning of the timepiece. The probability is much greater, of course, that the watch will be damaged. The watch is the result of a long tradition of highly skilled craftwork, and is not likely to be improved by such intervention. From the standpoint of earth's biological systems, the modern, industrial-consumer, wealth-seeking economy is wielding its technology in a similar way, with predictable disruptive and damaging consequences.

Barry Commoner was among the first to apply biological systems analysis to the dilemma modern economics has created within the human-earth relationship. This dilemma is clearly illustrated by the fact that in order to maintain the capital-driven economy under present conditions, it is necessary to increasingly damage the functional integrity of earth's ecosystems, and the biosphere as a whole. From the standpoint of science, this situation is devolutionary; from the standpoint of enlightened humanism, it is absurd; from the standpoint of religion, it is blasphemous.

Commoner's analysis of this dilemma is based on the "four laws of ecology:"

- Everything is connected to everything else.
- Everything must go somewhere.
- Nature [earth process] knows best.
- There is no such thing as a free lunch.

At first glance, these statements may appear simplistic, but they are solidly rooted in biological knowledge and in the thermodynamics of energy and matter. Taken together, they describe the ecological worldview and offer guidance for an ecologically based economic system.

In a second book, *The Poverty of Power: Energy and the Economic Crisis* (1976), Commoner develops a schematic formula that is both profound and memorable. Human settlements and social order depend on the operation of three interrelated systems:

- the planetary ecosystem,
- the human production system,
- the monetary exchange system.

Ecologically speaking, the interrelationship of these systems goes like this:

- The planetary ecosystem is the source of all materials and energy processes that support human life;
- The production system is the network of agricultural, industrial, and service activities that convert earth's materials, energy processes, and relationships into the wealth that sustains human settlements and social life.
- The monetary system represents the value of this wealth in ways that facilitate its exchange. It governs how this wealth is distributed and what is done with it.

In an ecologically coherent arrangement of these three systems, the governing influence would flow from the ecosystem, to the production system, and then to the monetary system. The governing integrity of the ecosystem would determine the design and operation of the production system. The stability and good service of the production system would determine the design and functioning of the monetary system.

Our contemporary economic reality, however, has the relationship of these three primary systems exactly the wrong way round. The wealth-seeking monetary system drives the production system into unlimited, consumption-based economic growth.

The production system, in order to meet this demand of the monetary system, generally operates without regard for the health and integrity of the ecosystem. The governing influence is flowing the wrong way, and the environmental crisis is the result. These comparative relationships can be diagrammed as follows:

Governing Influence >>>Outcome

Monetary System > Production System >
Ecosystem = Ecological Breakdown

Ecosystem > Production System > Monetary
System = Ecological Health

Barry Commoner's formula clearly illustrates the science-based approach to an ecological coherent economy, and the policy issues that must be addressed on the way to an ecologically sound way of life.

And finally, in this assembly, consideration must turn to the founding figure of modern ecological consciousness — Aldo Leopold. Leopold was a conservation biologist whose work encompassed field research, university teaching, public policy, and philosophical reflection that holds up the ecologically embedded basis of ethical development. He had the ability to frame his thoughts and insights in plain and memorable language. His best-known book, *A Sand County Almanac* (1949), collects his sketches from the field and his reflections on humanity's relationship with the land. One would never suppose from such a modest title that this book would become one of the prime sources of ecological consciousness in our time. Leopold's skill was twofold: he articulated a philosophy of ecology in a language of such quiet beauty that we get not only the conceptual understanding, but also the experience of the spirit in which he lived and worked.

In *A Sand County Almanac* he argued that the recognition of the "land community" is the preeminent discovery of modern science. This may seem a curious claim when such an array of dramatic discoveries, especially since his time, could be named to this honour. But if we think carefully about this, I believe we will see he is correct, and will continue to be correct for as long into the future as we care to imagine. The scientific recognition of the "land community," and the interdependencies that compose the ecological integrity of its functioning, is the fundamental context of human adaptation and wellbeing. *The same cannot be said for any other context of scientific discovery.*

Leopold suggested the next major step in the evolution of human moral sensibility would be the development of "the land ethic." He offered this formulation: "A thing is right when it tends to preserve the integrity, stability and beauty of the biotic community. It is wrong when it tends otherwise." Many volumes have since been written on the philosophy of ecology, but it is this simple statement, with its emphasis on the aesthetic factor in moral awakening, that has become the touchstone of the ecological worldview.

In brief, James Lovelock describes the emergence of life as an expression of earth-process, an expression that is characterized by a homeostatic regulatory function within biotic development itself that maintains the chemistry of earth's environment in the very condition required to enable the flourishing of life to continue. Understanding this ecological relationship inducts us into a great responsibility — the responsibility of being co-workers in the maintenance of the commonwealth of life. Thomas Berry describes the cultural context of this relationship, and details the range of activities that flow from the exercise of this responsibility. He calls these activities "the Great Work." Barry Commoner describes the processes and relationships that compose the organic world. He explains why the capital-driven market economy is deconstructing ecosystem integrity and cannot be sustained. He describes the ecological orientation toward economic adaptation. Aldo Leopold describes the enhancement of the human-earth relationship based on the emergence of "the land ethic." The land ethic, according to Leopold, comes into full effect when scientific knowledge and aesthetic experience of earth and its communities of life rise into respect, reverence, and love.

•   •   •

Such is the great circle in which the commonwealth of books and the commonwealth of the land converged in a community based farming vocation, which we developed and enjoyed on North Hill Farm until it was time for reasons of advancing age to make a change—a change that came to us in a surprising way.

Chapter Six

The Rebirth of a Bookseller
Penn Book Center, Philadelphia

Lord! When you sell a man a book you don't sell him just twelve ounces of paper, ink, and glue — you sell him a whole new life. Love and friendship and humour and ships at sea at night — there's all heaven and earth in a book, in a real book, I mean.

Christopher Morley
Parnassus on Wheels

Books: helping introverts avoid conversation since 1454.

Chalkboard sign at Books a Plenty
Tanranga, New Zealand

As the years of running a small-scale farm and market garden accumulated, our energy for keeping up the operation naturally diminished. North Hill Farm was a family endeavour, and Ellen and I could not have developed it as we did without the assistance of our sons, Eric and Brendan. They were both essential workers in the business, but we never expected they would necessarily take up farming as a way of life. They were both inclined toward artistic vocations, which was gratifying to see — Eric, to music and audio engineering, Brendan, to photography and graphic design.

The larger arc of our motivation had always been to establish and operate North Hill Farm as a platform from which to advance ecologically coherent, community-based, economic, social, and cultural development. From our first season as market gardeners, we set out to create a core group of local producers willing to work for the establishment of a Farm Market. Ellen became the chief organizer of this project and eventually the manager of the Woodstock Farm Market Cooperative through its early crucial years. The Market now has its own building on the waterfront in downtown Woodstock and is a six-day-a-week operation.

In addition, Ellen helped organize the New Brunswick Farm Market Association and conducted workshops around the province in communities where people wanted to start their own farm markets. In the 70s, "buy local," for which we beat the drum, seemed a quaint anachronism. Government policy, allied with the mindset of industrial scale agriculture, was "get big or get out." Fifty years later, small-scale producers have proliferated across the province and Farm Markets are operating in almost every community. "Buy local" has taken centre stage in the economic development policy of provincial and municipal governments. The former mayor of Woodstock describes our Farm Market as an "anchor institution" of the town. Although no longer vendors in the Market, Ellen and I remained on the Board of Directors until recently, and I now manage a thriving bookstall for the Market that displays the work of New Brunswick authors.

In the early years, it was particularly gratifying to see the way rural women took up the opportunity to create home-based, value-added food and craft products and sell them in the Farm Market. More than one husband was reluctant to have his wife enter the world of commerce, even at the level of the Farm Market, but once the supplementary income started rolling in this attitude often changed; husbands began assisting and enjoyed helping out at the market stall. The genius of a Farm Market is its niche in the community as both a social and commercial institution—just like a good bookstore.

During our farming years, I served on the Board of the local Credit Union, which grew from a small savings and loan operation to a full service financial institution. I worked with the public participation division of the federally sponsored Man and Resources Program, and in the same capacity with the St. John

River Basin Board. I was a local representative in the founding of the Valley Solid Waste Commission and continued to serve on its community advisory committee. A project that eventually established a local gristmill cooperative had its first meetings in our home at North Hill Farm. I served as the coordinator for an employment-training project for people who wanted to work but were hampered by various social and behavioural disabilities from getting and keeping a job. In addition, Ellen was invited by the regional manager of the provincial department of social services to initiate a homemakers project that would provide training for women to upgrade the food handling, nutritional, and childcare practices of family life. The project was eventually made a regular program of the local Red Cross office.

By the mid-1990s, Ellen and I had scaled back the farm operation to what we could handle on our own. We closed out the dairy goat and sheep raising part of the farm, sold the apple cider making business to another family, and concentrated our efforts on market garden and greenhouse production. Even so, it was clear the time was soon coming when a major transition would be needed. As we looked back over the trajectory of our efforts and assessed what our next move should be, the need to implement succession planning came firmly into focus. We decided to act peremptorily before the energy demands of the farm forced us to make a change. Family considerations loomed large in our feeling and thinking about what to do next. We both had aging parents—Ellen's in Virginia and my mother in Ohio—and we wanted to be closer to them in their last years.

Our sons were following out the opportunities of their vocational choices. Brendan, a graphic artist, had become a bookseller as well. After two years at the New Brunswick College of Craft and Design, he moved to Philadelphia and went to work at the Penn Book Center, which Achilles Nickles had taken over from his brother, Peter, after closing the Syracuse Book Center and moving back to New Jersey. Brendan eventually became the manager of a B. Dalton Bookseller at Moorestown Mall in New Jersey, but then moved to Borders' new flagship store when it opened on Walnut Street in Center City Philadelphia. He worked as the assistant events coordinator involving the production of the store's newsletter and running the in-store author events. By the time we were winding down the farm, Brendan, his child Jay and wife Rebecca, had moved to Birmingham, Alabama, where she had secured an appointment as the Shakespeare professor in the English Department at the University of Alabama. Brendan became a full-time dad and added to his graphic design training in classes at the university. Over the years he worked in graphic design, bookselling, and event lighting design.

Eric, after having completed degrees in music composition and studio engineering at Purchase College — the performing arts campus of the State University of New York system — was working as an adjunct instructor at Purchase, an audio engineer, and performing musician in the New York area.

We picked Philadelphia as a good place to relocate for bringing us closer to family. I would be an overnight train ride from my mother in Ohio. We would be a five-hour drive from Ellen's parents in Virginia. Alabama, though a long way from Philadelphia, was a lot closer than from New Brunswick. And Eric, living in Westchester County, New York, was close at hand. When the opportunity emerged to sell North Hill Farm to a family with young children who would value it in much the same way we had, we set our planning in motion.

An employment opportunity in program development was open at Pendle Hill, a Quaker study centre at Wallingford, near Philadelphia. In applying for the position I was required to provide a reference from a past employer. That presented a problem; I had been self-employed for most of the last three decades. Friends World College was now a program of Long Island University and there was no personnel carry-over from my time with the College. I had to reach all the way back to Achilles Nickles and our time together at the Syracuse Book Center to find an employer who could speak to their experience of me as an employee.

I wrote to Achilles telling him what was in the works for us around a move to Philadelphia and that he might get a call from

Pendle Hill with regard to my application for the position of program coordinator. As it turned out, on the very day I received a letter from Pendle Hill advising me the position had been filled, Achilles called to tell me that if I didn't get the position at Pendle Hill, the future of Penn Book Center had just taken a turn that included moving to a new location and redeveloping the store; he asked if I would be interested in joining the effort as manager.

Truly, it was like a summer day above the Arctic Circle where the sun dips briefly below the horizon and, minutes later, rises again into a clear sky. I never dreamt I would be able to return to the life of a bookseller in an academic community. After a quick consultation with Ellen, I said yes and we put the wheels in motion that took us to Philadelphia for what appeared to be the capstone opportunity of a bookselling vocation.

Achilles and Olga had been dealing with a situation that put the future of Penn Book Center in jeopardy. The University of Pennsylvania was evicting a whole block of small businesses along Walnut Street in the heart of the campus where Penn Book Center had been located for thirty years. The university was clearing the property to build — guess what — a luxurious new complex for the Wharton School of Business. The university was offering the evicted businesses alternative rental accommodations at various locations they also owned outside the core of the campus. They offered Penn Book Center a location blocks west on Walnut Street but so far removed from university activities and the natural flow of student and faculty traffic that the business would lose the key feature that had made it a success — a central campus location.

There was a good alternative location at the corner of 34th and Sansom, which had once been a Sam Goody record store, but the university's property office would not make it available to Penn Book Center. The word was they had a master plan of attracting upscale retail businesses to the available commercial space in the campus area in order to make it a more attractive shopping destination for wealthy visitors to the city. A bookstore, apparently, didn't fit the image of their dollar-studded development dream.

Rather than move the store to an unpromising location and endure the stress of uncertain redevelopment, Achilles and Olga decided to retire and began to sell off the store's inventory in preparation for closing down the business. When the word got out that Penn Book Center was closing down because the university was denying it a suitable location, a movement to save the store was started by faculty and students. Letters were written in support of the store and a petition was initiated that garnered hundreds of signatures.

As it turned out, an administrative angel appeared and secured the future of the store. Tom Lussenhop, the Managing Director of University Real Estate, and long time friend of Penn Book Center, intervened from the top and made the 34th Street location available. That's when Achilles called me and the die was cast for the redevelopment of the store and the rebirth of a bookseller.

•   •   •

We moved to Philadelphia in late October of 1998 and I spent the next two months taking the old store apart and reassembling it in the new location. Penn Book Center was the last tenant to vacate the block before demolition began. On the strength of reopening the first week in January, Achilles had taken faculty orders for spring semester course books, a trade Penn Book Center had successfully cultivated over the decades. Eric came from New York for the week between Christmas and New Years and we worked non-stop to mount the last of the slatwall panels and install the sales counter fixtures. We reopened on time amid boxes of books still to be shelved. Penn Book Center was back in business.

Achilles and I resumed our companionable owner/manager roles that had worked so well during our Syracuse years. As the owner of the business, all the financial matters were in his hands. My time and energy had the luxury of being devoted entirely to the intellectual and physical management of the store, which included category development and display arrangements, new book ordering, inventory control, and in-store promotion and marketing. Since much of the store's core stock had been sold off when it was expected to close, I first had the job of rebuilding the inventory needed by an academic bookstore. It was like my work as an acquisitions librarian at Friends World College, except this time I came to it with a deficit of knowledge about the current front-line intellectual and cultural worlds of academia.

I had not been intellectually idle during my vocational turn to farming, food systems, and community economic development. I could tell you more than you wanted to know about the eco-logically lethal practices of industrial agribusiness and the need for a rapid turn to a new kind of regenerative agriculture and local food system security. I could cite chapter and verse of the climate change story and the trajectory of catastrophe on which the industrial-consumer economies of the world were embarked, and on the need for the rapid deployment of renewable energy technologies. But I knew precious little about postmodern critical theory and the intellectual earthquake of cultural analysis known as "deconstructionism."

The work of Jacques Derrida, Giles Deleuze, Jean-Luc Nancy, Emmanuel Levinas, Slavoj Zizek, Richard Rorty, Ernesto Laclau, Paul Latour, Pierre Bourdieu, and Judith Butler, for example, had not come into view for me. I was familiar with Claude Levi-Straus, Michael Foucault, Marshall Sahlins, Marcel Mauss, Edmund Leach, Eric Wolf, Edward Evans-Pritchard, and Ernest Gellner, but some-thing beyond "structuralism" had come into play in cultural studies and the human sciences while I had been deep into earth-system science and ecological adaptation. As a bookseller to the academic community of an Ivy League university, I needed to understand how the intellectual winds of cultural analysis were now blowing. Clearly, I had some major catching up to do, even though I was fond of S. J. Perelman's remark—"How I wish I could keep up with the leaders of modern thought as they pass into oblivion."

Fortunately, I had a brilliant employee at hand who was thoroughly familiar with the leaders of post-modern critical theory and deconstructionist analysis. Eric Keenaghan was a graduate student in English at Temple University and a part-time employee of Penn Book Center. He stayed with us through the transition to the 34th Street location and became a mentor for me in understanding what was missing from my inventory of knowledge about current frontline thinkers in the humanities, plus the scholarship that had grown up around post-modern studies. I had never been well-disposed to modernism, so to pick up on work that moved beyond this cultural category interested me both personally and as a bookseller.

Eric was not given to extensive conversation, but he answered my questions with alacrity and precision and seemed to appreciate that I valued what he knew. I came to realize he had an extraordinary mental quickness and phenomenal memory. For example, when it came time to return unsold course books to publishers at the end of the semester, I noticed he prepared shipments more rapidly than I or other employees could manage. I asked him about this. He smiled, as if glad this had been noticed, and modestly replied that in preparing packing documents and shipping labels he didn't have to look up publishers' addresses — he remembered all of them. This same talent applied to his knowledge of contemporary intellectual and literary culture.

Eric Keenaghan is now an Associate Professor in the English Department at the Albany campus of the State University of New York. His scholarly publications and course descriptions display the intellectual brilliance and cultural savvy that was so helpful to me in curating the philosophy and critical theory sections of the new Penn Book Center.

•   •   •

It didn't take long after I began to rebuild the inventory of core books in the humanities, arts, and social sciences for conversations with Penn faculty to become a regular feature of my working day. Not only was I older than many of the professors that frequented the store, apparently Achilles had mentioned in conversation with them before my arrival that he was bringing in "a real bookman" as the new manager. At least, this is how it was reported to me as I began to enjoy the acquaintance of faculty with a strong loyalty to the store. Some of them had been employees of the store when they were graduate students and had on-going friendships with Achilles and Olga. Being welcomed into this network of scholars and bibliophiles was also a fast track into the intellectual milieu of the humanities, social science, and arts communities of the university.

Something quite extraordinary often happens when people who are bare acquaintances have a conversation about a mutually appreciated book, or when one of them introduces a book previously unknown to the other that instantly rings a bell and sparks an animated conversation. It's as if in a loose network of associations an island of common ground suddenly appears and a sense of affinity clicks into place that leaps across the space between them. There is something about the unexpected bonding over a book and its attributes that dispels a kind of loneliness and kindles a glow of solidarity and friendship. For most folks, this may happen once in a great while. For a bookseller, who is open to the opportunity, it happens with regularity and is why bookstores generate such rich intellectual and social relationships. I was familiar with this feature of bookstore management, but my ten years at Penn Book Center added significantly to the breadth of these serendipitous associations.

For example, I remember the day Susan Stewart came into the store with a clothbound copy of her new book, *Poetry and the Fate of the Senses*, and presented it to me. I had been reading her poetry, but did not have a full sense of her literary research and cultural analysis. Our order of her new book in the paperback edition from the University of Chicago Press had not yet arrived so this was the first I had seen it. I thought perhaps she was just showing it to me, but when I opened it I found this inscription;

> *In cloth for Keith*
> *who keeps*
> *the flame*
> *at 34th and Sansom!*
>
> *Deepest thanks & much affection. Susan*

I had known this book was in preparation and had expressed an interest in its theme. We shared the apprehension that so much about the way of life subsumed in the industrial-consumer economy was withering the sensuous vitality of the human-earth relationship and that a huge swath of survival skills both physical and spiritual were being lost. I was deeply touched by her gift of recognition and the presentation of this book.

Susan was a good friend of Achilles and Olga as well and we were all a bit bereft when she told us she had taken a new appointment at Princeton. In one of the last conversations we had before the move, she made a point to tell me about the work of her good friend and colleague at Stanford, Robert Pogue Harrison. He had published *Forests: The Shadow of Civilization* in 1992, the first of a trilogy project. *The Dominion of the Dead* was soon to be released (2003), and *Gardens: An Essay on the Human Condition* would follow in due course. (It appeared in 2008.) She thought this major project of cultural analysis would interest me for both the depth of its insight into the human-earth relationship and for the grace and beauty of the writing.

Her sense of the appeal Harrison's work would have for me couldn't have been more perfectly calibrated. There are certain books that once read I know I will be rereading for the rest of my life. Harrison's books have joined this select company. I have kept in touch with Susan and she recently let me know about the publication of her latest book, *The Ruins Lesson: Meaning and Material in Western Culture*. I have it on the bench by my fireside chair with a bookmark that has already travelled a quarter of the way into the text.

And then there was Ian McHarg, the doyen of landscape architecture who founded a pioneering department for this discipline at Penn in 1954 and chaired it until 1968. I had long known of his work and had a first edition of his 1969 magnum opus, *Design with Nature*. I knew of his association with the university, but had no idea he was still around and an active presence on campus. He was also a friend of Penn Book Center and Achilles introduced us soon after the store reopened. I immediately saw he was a charismatic character and great storyteller—the kind of person you mostly listened to with fascination and plied with an occasional, stimulating question.

But what really got us on the same wavelength was that in curating the store's inventory I early on added a new section devoted to landscape architecture. It turned into a great selection of books and got the attention of faculty and students at Penn Design, which the department of landscape architecture and city planning was now called. John Dixon Hunt, Laurie Olin, and David Leatherbarrow were central figures in the department at this time and their books alone added substantially to the new section's core inventory. When building up a new category of books, there's no better source of information than faculty authors whose books you already have on display. Ian McHarg was especially responsive to my initiative.

The high point of our association came in December of 1999 when he came in to the store waving a letter he had just received from Japan. Out of the blue, The Science and Technology Foundation of Japan had awarded him the Japan Prize in recognition of his contribution to urban landscape design and city planning. The award ceremony was scheduled for April 2000 in Tokyo at which time he would be presented with the Japan Prize Medal and the sum of $500,000.

He showed me the letter. I asked him if I could make a copy and enlarge it to use as a centrepiece in a window display of his books and others from the landscape architecture section. He beamed his approval and appreciation. The next day Penn Book Center's large window fronting 34th Street held an eye-catching display in honour of Ian McHarg and the legacy of his life's work, including a copy of *VIA 1, Ecology in Design,* from my personal library. This 1968 student publication of the Graduate School of Fine Arts at the University of Pennsylvania is an oversize compendium of photographs and landscape design studies anchored by a major contribution from McHarg. When I pointed out the inclusion of this vintage publication in the display, he said, "Where did you get that? I don't even have a copy." He was touched by my effort and I was pleased to have a part in promoting the discipline on which, in large part, hangs the future of the human-earth relationship. Sadly, I saw Ian McHarg only a few times after his trip to Japan for the award ceremony. He was not well and, failing rapidly, died in March of 2001.

As I became acquainted with an increasing number of Penn faculty and graduate students, my ability to build up the store's inventory in a way that matched their interests steadily improved. It's a rare professor or graduate scholar that is not a book collector. The opportunity to surprise and delight by ordering in and displaying new titles in their disciplines is an especially satisfying bookstore routine. When space is limited, as it always is, a carefully curated inventory is both a thoughtful service and smart marketing.

I especially remember the day Arthur Waldron — a brilliant and recently arrived addition to the history department — stood in the middle of the main floor and declared in a booming voice, "The thing I like about this store is that all the books are ones I want to know about and there are none of the ones I don't want to know about." He then added there were only two other bookshops in the world that commanded his interest in the same way — one in Paris and one in London. While I recognized an element of self-aggrandizement in such a statement, it certainly summed up and confirmed my curatorial ambition for Penn Book Center. I thereafter took full conversational advantage of Professor Waldron's book loving ebullience.

Dan Traister, then Curator of the Rare Book and Manuscript Library at Penn's Van Pelt-Dietrich Library, was not only one of the store's best customers, he had a talent for browsing that surpassed even my level of accomplishment in the field. He quickly saw and appreciated what I was doing in redeveloping Penn Book Center. It was a rare week we did not see Dan coming through the door on several different days. He made a habit not only of keeping a watchful eye on the ever-changing displays of new books but systematically browsed the subject sections of the entire store. He was interested in most everything and regularly found another book or two, which he either purchased or handed across the counter to be placed on his stack of books being held for later acquisition.

Dan joked about being mindful of the number of books he brought home at the same time. At one point he mentioned the need to build an addition on his house to hold his growing collection of books. I don't remember whether this was also a joke or if it really happened. In any event, although he regularly sorted through his reserve of books and made selections for purchase, the stack on hold never diminished. Some book collectors are reticent about their habit; Dan was the opposite and for the decade of our association was a true ally in supporting and advancing my mission for Penn Book Center.

Andrew Lamas, another good friend of the store, was also a man on a mission. We connected over our mutual interest and similar histories working with cooperatives to advance community development and economic democracy. He was a close student of Herbert Marcuse, which rang a bell with me and was passionate about issues of social and economic justice. Beyond his teaching in Penn's Urban Studies Program, Andy was organizationally active in a variety of projects dedicated to self-help economic development. He was that rare blend of academic and activist.

Several years after I had retired from Penn Book Center, I was again visiting the store as I regularly did whenever in Philadelphia. Before entering, I was studying the window displays on Sansom Street, when Andy Lamas comes walking down the hill. He asked what I was now doing and we struck up a conversation like we had been only temporarily interrupted. He offered to take me to lunch at the White Dog Café just up Sansom and we spent an intense and enjoyable hour in conversation about substantial issues of social justice and the still crying need for revolutionary action against capitalism's hegemony.

I remember he chided me a bit for my community garden, renewable energy, and farm market work not being sufficiently radical. I countered by reminding him I lived in a country where social democracy was truly cherished and the national motto was "peace, order, and good government" rather than the individualistic mantra of "life, liberty, and the pursuit of happiness." He understood the difference but "stuck to his guns," so-to-speak, on the need to refuse capitalism's hegemony, even in Canada. I conceded the point. I see from its website that Andy was a founding Board member of the International Herbert Marcuse Society, on which he continues to serve. This means the ethos of the "Great Refusal" that Marcuse championed still flourishes.

When Michael Eric Dyson came to Penn on a temporary appointment, he hit the campus like a whirlwind. At least that's how it seemed when he first came to Penn Book Center and discovered our African-American Studies section. With running commentary partly to the booksellers on hand and partly, it seemed, to the Universe in general, he proceeded to pick out volume after volume and pile them on the sales counter in a double stack until the clerk on duty disappeared behind a wall of books.

Those who have heard Michael Eric Dyson hold forth from a podium, or have been a student in one of his classes, or heard him interviewed on TV news know what a master of verbal delivery he is. He has the same rhetorical gift as Jesse Jackson but ramped up a notch in the torrent of its non-stop flow. Non-stop is not quite right because in my experience he was amenable to answering questions, which, of course, was my forte as a bookseller always on the lookout for good advice on important titles that may have escaped my notice.

The books Dyson piled up on that first visit tallied out at over $500 even with the faculty discount deducted, and our African-American Studies section looked a shambles — big gaps on the shelves with books falling over sideways. I prided myself on the neatness of my displays, but I did not complain about the effect of this sales event. I set to work reordering the missing titles and, thanks to Ingram Books' excellent distribution service to the trade, the section was restored to a respectable appearance within a week.

But Michael Dyson wasn't done. He was soon back in the store sweeping through other sections and piling up his purchases to the level of several hundred dollars per visit. This level of purchasing eventually tapered off as he got to the end of mining the sections that interested him. During the year's time he was at Penn we had the benefit of not only his credit card but of his eloquent commentary on what he was reading. I had the impression he was reading almost as fast as he was purchasing.

Peter Conn was also a good friend of the store. By vocation he was an English professor but when I met him he was serving as Dean of the University. Although he never mentioned it, I had the impression he was among those in high places that went to bat for the Book Center when the question of relocation was on the line. My first encounter with him went a bit oddly. I was at the sales counter when he laid down several books for purchase. I knew who he was and deducted the customary faculty discount. At that point, he intervened, sharply instructing me in an annoyed manner that he did not take the faculty discount and never had. It was as though he thought I should know this was his practice. When he saw I was taken aback, he softened and explained it was his policy to pay the full price for his purchases because he wanted to do everything he could to make sure Penn Book Center survived. I thanked him for his consideration.

Peter Conn later kept us apprised of his son's progress toward the completion of a major book on "Native Americans" in American history. When the University of Chicago Press published Steven Conn's book in 2004, he credited his father for an important role in its final preparation. Although Steven was a history professor at Ohio State University, we gave his book the same level of promotion we gave new books by Penn authors. *History's Shadow: Native Americans and Historical Consciousness in the Nineteenth Century* was received as an outstanding contribution to its field by the profession. Steven Conn visited Penn and the Penn Book Center when his book was published and, thanks partly to his father's effective promotion, we sold a satisfying number of copies.

• • •

As the store became fully stocked and running smoothly, I began to widen my association with key faculty and departmental administrators. The result was an increasing number of requests to provide and host book displays at conferences, guest lecture events, and Penn author book launches. For example, the Center for Bioethics established at Penn by Arthur Caplan regularly convened high profile conferences at which we displayed and sold the steadily increasing number of titles being published in this controversial and expanding field of study and research. Caplan was a skilled promoter and a prolific writer who appreciated the marketing expertise we brought to his events. And, of course, we appreciated the sales and maintained a comprehensive Bioethics section in the store.

In the same way, our connection with Renée Fox, a leading figure in the sociology of medicine, provided the opportunity to host book displays at conferences and lectures. Her research had started in Europe and then shifted to Central Africa. Later, her studies focused on the work of Médecins Sans Frontiéres, which led to projects in Siberia, Chechnya, Dagestan, and later in South Africa in response to the HIV outbreak. Unlike some social science scholars who idle back to a less strenuous professional life after completing a major research project, Renée Fox's commitment to frontline research was life long. Professionals in the field who had been her students were especially active in honouring her as she approached retirement, which culminated in a major festschrift-like event held in a Philadelphia Center City hotel. There was an unusual quality of feeling and sense of care for the human condition in her work that was clearly evident in those who gathered to honour her. In preparing for this event, she made sure we had the information needed to access not only her publications but also those of her former students and colleagues.

There often comes a point when being engaged as a bookseller in events like these that you realize the opportunity has provided an intense and privileged insight into a field of scholarship and its network of both professional and personal relationships. To paraphrase Isaac Walton's famous aphorism, "It is not all of fishing to fish," I can say it is not all of bookselling to sell books. There is a circular flow in the intellectual and cultural economy of bookselling that rebounds to the benefit of the bookseller as well as to those who purchase books. It's a regular feature of the sociology of bookstores but leaps to a new level when bookselling at conferences.

Invitations to participate in such events increased and I developed a system of response that became a major outreach feature of Penn Book Center. With the frequency of special lectures, daylong workshops, and weekend conferences that occur at Penn, my monthly calendars were dotted with bookselling events large and small.

The largest lecture event at which we served as the bookseller was for Wangari Maathai, the Kenyan environmental, social justice, and political activist who was awarded the Nobel Peace Prize in 2004. With the publication of her 2006 memoir, *Unbowed* by Alfred Knopf Books, she was on tour in North America. We were given short notice on the event but a call to Random House made sure the books arrived in time for her appearance at Penn. It's hard to judge the likely sales for this level of event and you don't want to run short. On the other hand, an over estimate requires returning the surplus, which means eating the shipping costs and eroding profit. I knew the venue for the lecture was a five hundred-seat auditorium and figured it would be filled, which, when the night came, it was. I ordered two hundred books. Normally, an event is a success if the rate of sales equals a third of the audience. I calculated this event might be above that rate. Two hundred turned out to be the right number. With follow-up sales at the store, only a few copies were eventually returned to Random House.

Another event of major significance was the Penn launch of the first edition of *Africana: The Encyclopedia of African and African American Experience.* The project that produced this 2144 page book had been organized and coordinated by the editors, Kwame Anthony Appiah (Princeton) and Henry Louis Gates (Harvard). We had been invited by the African American Studies Program at Penn to serve as bookseller for the launch event at which Gates was to be the featured speaker. With what we hoped would be an adequate number of books, I showed up well in advance of the afternoon starting time because I knew the layout of the large lecture hall presented a problem for good display. Sure enough, when I arrived the organizers had the book display table set up at the back of the hall. The problem was the only doors in and out of the room were set midway in the long right hand wall. There would be no natural flow of traffic past a book table at the back of the room.

I sought out the person who was in charge of arrangements and explained my concern. I wanted to be set up in the hallway just outside the two doorways through which everyone attending would enter and exit. My request was denied. He thought setting up there would impede traffic flow. Within minutes, Henry Louis Gates arrived in the company of university administrators and began to check out the arrangements for the event including the display and sales arrangements for the book. I was introduced to him as the bookseller and immediately saw the opportunity to enlist him in addressing the display problem.

In a flash, he understood and took command with a directive to the logistics person that the book table should be relocated to the space between the doors in the hallway. I had previously heard his friends refer to him as Skip Gates and could now see how his quick manner of commanding attentiveness would have earned him this nickname. He even helped move the boxes of books to the new location. The space required using a smaller table for display and stacking up the boxes against the wall behind us, but we made it work and sold nearly all the books.

A conference on women and literature, organized by English Professor Phyllis Rackin, provided another memorable bookselling experience. Margaret Atwood was the keynote speaker. We were invited to set up a display of her books, which was not as easy as it sounds. How to choose from the large array of titles available? I put together a selection from what we had in stock at the store, ordered in significant missing titles, and featured her most recent book, *The Tent* — an idiosyncratic collection of thirty-five Atwood vignettes. The display covered an eight-foot table set up in the lobby of the lecture hall where she would be speaking.

Shortly before the afternoon event was due to begin, Ms. Atwood, accompanied by Professor Rackin, and a bevy of graduate students, came through the double door entrance. Professor Rackin and her troupe turned right toward the lecture hall but Margaret Atwood made a beeline for the book-table. She surveyed the lot and looking up said, "This is the best display of my books I've seen in some time. Thank you for your effort."

This was quite remarkable. In my years of experience, celebrity authors rarely paid attention to the bookseller. They sweep into the venue surrounded by the event host and eager acolytes. Ah ha, I thought, Margaret Atwood is a Canadian; she's different. But that was only the beginning. Her manner was so inviting I couldn't help but express my admiration for the large enamel brooch she was wearing; it was the size of a silver dollar and bore the image of Queen Elizabeth. She looked at me quizzically, and I quickly added, "I'm from New Brunswick." She broke into a smile and we exchanged a bit more Canadian talk before her host urged her on to the lecture hall. I kept thinking, what kind of sly humour is this? Margaret Atwood shows up at a feminist conference wearing an enormous brooch displaying the image of the Queen of England, indeed, of the Commonwealth. I've been smiling at the memory of the incident ever since.

One of the most soulful encounters of my bookselling days occurred when we were asked by the Humanities Forum at the University of Pennsylvania to provide the book service for the visit and reading of Palestinian poet, Taha Muhammad Ali. The event was held at 3619 Locust Walk, which is a stately old house that remained intact as the university campus grew around it and repurposed the facility instead of tearing it down. The first floor opened into a meeting room that nicely accommodated an audience of up to thirty or so for the literary readings regularly held there.

Shortly before the visit of Ali, Sam Hamill, co-founder of Copper Canyon Press, had given a reading at this venue. It was a pleasure meeting him, holding a brief conversation, and getting a feel for why this man from a Utah farm childhood credits Gary Snyder's poetry for saving his life. All this was like a comfortable echo chamber of my own cultural experience, although I hadn't needed the rescuing that Sam Hamill ascribed to Snyder's mentoring influence.

The meeting with Taha Muhammad Ali was radically different. His poetry, his persona, his story launched us into an unforgettable cross-cultural experience. Here was a man in his 70s, whose whole life mirrored the dispossession of family, village, and people from house, land, and a self-provisioning economy. Yet he had endured and educated himself in classic Arabic literature and the modern forms of poetry and story telling. Ali had emerged from his experience with a poetic voice of such direct resonance that even in translation it brought the listener bolt upright with its painful honesty and disarming humour.

Ali was on a North American tour with his first book to be translated into English. The book, titled *Never Mind*, was beautifully designed and printed by Ibis Edition in Jerusalem. It was a 5 by 6¼ inch trim size with French flaps—just the size to easily slip in a coat pocket and keep close at hand. I ordered twenty-five copies from the American distributor and read the poems before the event so I had a feeling for what was to come. But I was not prepared for what happened next.

After the reading, and after the lingering conversations with folks in attendance, Ali came to my book table at the rear of the room. The display of books I had initially laid out had considerably diminished. The sales had been brisk. I was pleased and so was Ali. He had noticed. He leaned over the table, took one of my hands in both of his, and thanked me with what seemed rising emotion. He was a large, rugged face man with a gentle manner. I stood up, put my other hand on his and thanked him for being here and sharing his moving poetry. We stood there leaning toward each other, softly shaking our clasped hands. He then said, "I want to give you something." Our hands unclasped. He drew a wallet from his pocket, opened it, took out a five-dollar bill, and put in my hand. Of course, I protested, saying, "No, no, I don't need to be paid. I'm here for my bookstore to sell your book and happy to do so."

Instantly, I knew that wouldn't do. I had misread the situation. This was not payment, this was a gesture of reciprocity and the only thing at hand to fulfill this ingrained cultural custom was money. I had done something for him that was probably of greater value than I realized, and there was no way I could, or should, prevent him from doing something for me in return. I shifted gears and thanked him for his appreciation for my bookselling service. After a few more words together, I walked with him to his host waiting by the door. Again we clasped hands before they departed. I have never forgotten this encounter. The memory of it often comes unbidden and a sense of solidarity across cultures lights up in my mind as one of things this sad world is most in need of.

In preparing to tell this story I took my copy of *Never Mind* from the shelf and found the flyer for Ali's reading event tucked inside. When I unfolded it, there was the five-dollar bill he had given me, now a priceless memento. The information at the bottom of the flyer was even more surprising. Taha Muhammad Ali's reading event at Penn had been co-sponsored by the Consulate General of Israel in Philadelphia, the Middle East Center, and the Jewish Studies Program of the University of Pennsylvania. Cross-cultural solidarity was more in evidence in this event than I had realized.

•　　•　　•

Our book service was recruited for events outside the Penn system as well. For example, we provided book service to a national conference on urban forestry, for the annual conference of the American Library Association when it was held in Philadelphia, and for numerous lecture events at Drexel University, which was adjacent to the Penn campus. In addition, an extraordinary and sustained book service relationship was established with Metanexus Institute.

Metanexus started out in the 90s as the Philadelphia Center for Religion and Science (PCRS), an initiative of William Grassie with the assistance of paleontologist Peter Dodson, neuroscientist

Andrew Newberg, and anthropologist Soloman Katz, all associated with the University of Pennsylvania. Billy Grassie — as he was known in those days — was working on a PhD in religion at Temple University but was an activist at heart. As a young man of the 60s he had been engaged in peace education and international citizen diplomacy with the Nuclear Freeze Movement and with the American Friends Service Committee — a Quaker peace and social justice organization. He was now interested in generating a context in which a dialogue between science and religion contributed to a new era of human understanding and cross-cultural global solidarity.

His efforts attracted the support of the Templeton Foundation. With major grants in hand PCRS was renamed Metanexus Institute and began an ambitious, international, cross-disciplinary program of "constructive engagement of religion and science" that drew both scientists and theologians to weeklong conferences. Leading scholars from universities and colleges worldwide where science and religion studies were at that time emerging, responded to the conferences.

For five years, these summer conferences grew to the point where they attracted hundreds of participants. They were truly multi-cultural and cross disciplinary events, attracting scholars and researchers from the Middle East, South Asia, Korea, and Japan. Islamic scholarship in science and religion was well represented. Catholic theologians in the tradition of Teilhard de Chardin were enthusiastic participants. Liberal religion theologians who had survived the "death of God" era, along with biologists and cosmologists, found the Metanexus approach to building cross-disciplinary dialogue stimulating and productive. William Grassie assembled an organizational team that made this formidable project work, but it was his ability to articulate the ethos of the quest for human self-understanding within the new story of an evolving universe that guided the year-by-year development of Metanexus programs.

From the start, Penn Book Center was asked to provide book service to these conferences and act as a bibliographic consultant.

Many of the conference participants had never had access to the range of books we brought to these events. As the scale of the conferences expanded, so did our book service, which, I was told more than once, was a feature of the conferences that repeat attenders looked forward to. A number of participants made substantial purchases for the libraries of the institutions with which they were associated. Our week's sales at the third annual conference totalled nearly $30,000.

Projects like this, that catch a moment of substantial cultural interest and experience rapid growth, tend to plateau and then taper off to a transition phase. Metanexus was no exception. William Grassie was sensitively aware of this organizational dynamic. In year five of the large conference phase, he announced that, while still committed to the mission of Metanexus, he was stepping back and passing the leadership on to his organizational colleagues. He simultaneously secured a Fulbright Teaching Fellowship at a university in Sri Lanka. His 2010 book, *The New Science of Religion*, is a comprehensive articulation of the engagement of science and religion that permeated the Metanexus interdisciplinary conferences.

Metanexus was a shooting star in a golden moment of cultural convergence. Penn Book Center's book and bibliographic service was a significant feature of its trajectory and a relationship that was mutually beneficial to both parties. Metanexus Institute as an on-going educational organization eventually closed down but the name and core mission was later picked up again by William Grassie and now functions under his direction in the exploration of foundational questions within the narrative context of what has come to be called "Big History."

•　•　•

In 2006, Achilles and Olga were again ready to retire and advertised the Penn Book Center for sale, which left me wondering what the change would mean for me. Fortunately, the ideal couple stepped up to the opportunity and purchased the business. Michael Row was a PhD graduate of Penn's Wharton School of Business who had subsequently done well in the information technology boom. Ashley Montagu was a PhD Penn graduate in English. They had two young children and were looking for a local business opportunity in which they could work together. Penn Book Center was the perfect fit for them and their combination of skills and expertise were ideally suited for the business. Ashley was a literary and book loving person. Michael was a business management person with high-level proficiency in digital technology. They made me promise to stay with them until they got their bookstore management feet under them. This was fine with me and we spent the next two years in a congenial period of transition.

Ashley's main job was to take over the book buying and inventory management role as well as promotion, marketing, and floor management. Michael's task, in addition to the financial management of the business, was to computerize the whole operation. I knew this would be an important upgrade in efficient management of the store but the prospect set me to wondering about my ability to adapt. Michael was an action person; when he made a decision, the wheels of implementation immediately began to roll. He picked up on my apprehension and offered this reassurance; "Keith, I know you're an analog person, not a digital person. What I want to do is get as much of what is in your head into the computer as is possible, and I'll show you how we'll do it."

He then explained he wanted me to go through the store's entire inventory and categorize each title in one of three ways—canonical, significant, or marginal. Canonical meant the title should always be reordered and kept in stock. Significant meant that a decision should be made about whether or not to reorder. Marginal meant do not reorder. He set me up with a computer and showed me how to create this inventory database. I worked with Ashley as she stepped into the new book buying role and said my fond farewells to the faithfully appearing sales reps, a number of whom had regularly taken me out to lunch when they made their calls and happily put me on their list for receiving complimentary copies of books in which I was particularly interested. My library now includes a significant sprinkling of books obtained in this way.

I regularly pull a book from the shelf for reading or to check a reference and, finding the publisher's complimentary card inside the front cover, roll back in memory to those good days at Penn Book Center. After a two-year transition period, I became sufficiently marginal to the operation that I could step out of the picture and retire from bookselling with a satisfied mind.

I can't leave this tale of a bookseller reborn without a tip of the hat to my floor-managing assistant, Bill Green. Bill was a bookselling colleague of my son, Brendan, at the Borders bookstore when it opened in Center City. It was a great day when he applied for a job at the Penn Book Center. Bill was truly a book person, well read in literary fiction and able to engage customers in intelligent conversation on any subject. He was intellectually curious, had a gentle sense of humour always close to the surface, and could be depended on to handle well any situation that arose in the management of the store. People like Bill Green in the bookstore business are a large part of what makes it such a unique and socially rewarding work environment.

• • •

I no longer have the bookstore life that started so long ago and far away with The Paper Place in Iowa City, and then came back to me for another decade at Penn Book Center in Philadelphia. But I have a considerable library and when I sit down to ponder on things in its presence, or even to just have a nap, its ambiance brings up happy memories of my years as a bookseller. The older I get, the more I take to heart the wise words of Viktor Frankl in *Man's Search for Meaning*: "Memories are real possessions."

When I said "yes" to Achilles's question about wanting to work at The Paper Place, the course of our family life entered a trajectory of relationships that has carried us through the ensuing years with a remarkable degree of coherence. There is something about working in the commonwealth of books that can touch the sense of vocation like no other business. I think it is precisely the *spiritus mundi* that comes alive when one is immersed in the literature and scholarship of the human venture that makes the difference.

A good bookstore is inhabited. Minds and souls of the past and present commingle on the shelves and in the aisles. The conversation of the ages carries on in a timeless way. There is a factor of accompaniment and guidance that is available from being surrounded and on close terms with the wisdom and heartbreak of the human condition. The recorded struggle to comprehend and the language that praises the beauty of the world are always close at hand.

•　　•　　•

When we moved to Philadelphia in 1998 we didn't know what our situation after retirement might be. During our decade in the city, Ellen worked as the Executive Assistant to the General Secretary of Friends General Conference, which was a significant and satisfying use of her organizational and administrative skills. (Friends General Conference is a national Quaker organization and "General Secretary" is the Quaker name for its Executive Director). In 2003, I presented a prospectus for a Quaker "think tank" to an invited weekend gathering of thirty-six Quaker econ-omists, ecologists, and public policy professionals that resulted in the establishment of Quaker Institute for the Future. This development set the stage for my move into book publishing.

By 2006, however, we knew that returning to New Brunswick was the right move. More than once when visiting Woodstock during the time we were living in Philadelphia, we would meet people on the street who would say, "Oh, you're home for a visit." That was striking. They might have said, "Oh, you're back for a visit." But they said "home." That touched us and made us realize, yes, this is our home place. With that clarity in mind, we purchased a lovely 1866 heritage house located within walking distance of the library, the post office, and the Farm Market in the town of Woodstock. It sits on a double lot with a small copse of trees at the back and a large garden in front. Ah, I thought, retirement at last. I should have known better. The commonwealth of books had one more call.

Chapter Seven

Publishing the Literature of Place
Chapel Street Editions
Woodstock, New Brunswick

[Publishing] ... is a vocation, you feel you're doing
something ... important, and it's worth sacrificing for,
because without books we wouldn't know who we were.

Jason Epstein
Editorial Director, Random House
Co-founder, New York Review of Books

When we decamped from North Hill Farm in the wooded hills of the Wolastoq watershed to a lovely garden apartment just off Rittenhouse Square in Center City Philadelphia for a decade of immersion in the bookstore business, I carried with me the germ of an idea that eventually became a book publishing project.

Our elderly neighbour and sheep farming friend, Murray Hubbard, had written and self-published a small book about the history of Speerville, the settlement in which both our farms were located. He titled his book *How Well I Remember* and placed an epigraph from Emerson on the cover; "The years teach what the days never know."

Murray was an unusual farmer. He was self-educated in literature and natural history to a degree that it was a rare conversation with him that did not come up with a nugget of wisdom or angle of insight worth pondering. Although a sheep farmer by vocation, he was a horticulturist and gardener at heart. As a child, his mother had taught him the Latin names for plants.

He was a lay reader in his rural Anglican Church. When he spoke, he held forth in the cadences of Elizabethan English. He wrote in much the same way — and Murray was a writer.

In addition to his book on local history, Murray Hubbard had written a regular column for the local newspaper. His column observed and commented on the comings and goings of the seasons, the fate and fortunes of farm and garden life throughout our region. His writing was sprinkled with historical anecdotes and an appreciation of rural heritage and traditions. Murray titled his column, "The Countryman" which he took from a charmingly old fashioned journal of country life published in England to which he had long subscribed and read with delight.

My idea for a book publishing project was to produce a volume of Murray's best Countryman columns; they were all preserved on microfiche in our local library. By the late 90s I had not yet acted on this idea and we were now moving to Philadelphia. I passed the idea on to George Peabody, a writer and editor who had returned to Woodstock from British Columbia and was also interested in heritage preservation and the literature of place. George had other projects in the works and, in 2008, when we returned to Woodstock, he jokingly handed the Murray Hubbard project back to me. This was the germ of an idea that led Ellen and I, along with our son, Brendan, to create Chapel Street Editions (CSE), a small, non-profit publishing company devoted to the literature of place. However, we didn't start with the Murray Hubbard Countryman book; that one is still in the wings. We started with other opportunities to advance the literary heritage of our region — a story to which I will return.

My first step into book publishing came in the last two years of our sojourn in Philadelphia. With the creation of Quaker Institute for the Future (QIF) in 2003, an association of scholar-activists converged to address the spiralling crisis of the conflict between the growth-insistent economy and the ecological integrity of earth's biosphere.

Our core mission was to compile and distill the research findings that describe this conflict and to prepare and publish reports that offer both personal and public policy guidance for creating an ecologically integrated economy—an economy built up around a mutually enhancing human-earth relationship. Toward that end, QIF initiated The Moral Economy Project with the goal of producing a flagship book for the Institute. A founding Board member, Peter G. Brown, took the lead and secured a private grant to fund what turned out to be a three year program of research, workshops, drafting, focus group review, redrafting, and book publication. The project culminated with the Moral Economy Symposium held over three days at the University of Montreal and attended by over two hundred participants.

The book that was published was collaboratively created by five authors, of which I was one. In addition, I took on an editing task that drew on my experience in the book business and provided a good introduction to this midwife role in creating a book. What we produced, however, was a different kind of book than the one originally imagined. The manuscript had a roller-coaster journey.

About a year and half into the project, Peter Brown took all the material that had been created by the workshops, weekend conferences, and consultations and drafted a manuscript. It set out five basic questions about the economy: What is an economy for? How does it work? How big is too big? What's fair? How can it best be governed? All this, Peter packed into a long introductory chapter and then proceeded to a detailed discussion of various related issues and themes in subsequent chapters. With this manuscript in hand, he convened several focus groups composed of professional colleagues. I attended the one he convened at the University of Maryland where he had been a Professor of Public Policy in the School of Public Affairs, and had established the School's Environmental Policy Programs. In addition, he had the distinction of having recruited Herman Daly, a senior scholar in the field of ecological economics, to the University of Maryland, which, of course, meant this august personage was sitting at the head of the table when our focus group convened.

Each of the eight participants provided their assessment of the manuscript, which was mostly positive but with some reservation about its density and a question about the audience for whom it was being written. One respondent said that in revising the manuscript we should think about writing it for first year university and college students. If we used that audience as a guide, the book would be accessible to the general reader. That proved to be excellent advice. A professor of law said she had been looking for a book like this for her course on International Environmental Governance and if we get this book published she would use it. That was encouraging.

Herman Daly spoke last. He looked at Peter and said, "I think this manuscript should be shredded." Peter, who knew Herman well, didn't know what to say, but something in the manner of how this blow was delivered signalled there was more to come. Sure enough, Herman followed up by saying, "This book is so important you should start again and rewrite it." So the focus group was a success and we had our marching orders.

I had my reservations as well, which I now shared with Peter after the focus group disbanded. He was a good writer but had a penchant for acerbic phrases when he wanted to give particular emphasis to the wilful stupidities and criminal greed of capitalism's worst excesses. I told him I didn't disagree with anything he'd written, but in the interest of appealing to the range of readers we wanted the book to reach there were ways of saying what he wanted to say that would come across better than the sharp rhetorical jabs that punctuated the current manuscript. I wasn't sure how he would react, but he was grateful I had brought this up and replied; "OK, Keith, take out all the burrs and thistles." With this, I had my editing orders and didn't hesitate. Thereafter, Peter and I worked closely, along with Geoffrey Garver, John Howell, and Steve Szeghi on rewriting the manuscript.

Another rewriting instruction came from the editor at Berrett-Koehler Publishers. Peter had engaged the interest of B-K in the book and was working with senior editor, Johanna Vondeling. She observed that asking and answering the five questions dealt with in the first chapter is the core message of the book. She told us that if we write one chapter on each question and do it in two hundred pages, "that's the book I want to publish." This was a stroke of editorial genius that clarified our rewriting task. The chapters were parcelled out, drafted, shared around, revised, shared again, further revised, and finally edited to achieve a unified voice.

Johanna was happy with the result. But we had not yet settled on a title and B-K was ready to go to print. She set up a conference call in which we all participated. We had to come up with a title. After considering several unsatisfactory options, she consolidated our attention by saying,

> All the way through this book you repeatedly refer to the concept of "right relationship." It's central to your whole way of thinking about what makes for a moral economy. How about using it for the title of the book?

A silence ensued, but it was not an uncomfortable silence. Another stroke of editorial genius had been offered. I was the first to speak.

> That's perfect, but we need a subtitle that's equally prominent on the cover to let people know what the book is about. Otherwise it will be in danger of being shelved in bookstores with books on marriage counselling. How about *Building a Whole Earth Economy* as a subtitle?

From five phones, laughter, and then unanimous ascent rolled in. We had our title and subtitle.

Johanna wound up the call by saying, "Now I want you guys to know you have done *half* the work it takes to make a successful book." Wait a minute, we had worked on this book for two years; but we all knew she was right and perhaps exaggerating only a bit about the promotion and marketing effort that lay ahead. The economy of books is part of the attention economy and getting *Right Relationship* noticed by the people we wanted to read it and be influenced by its message required strategic post-launch planning and committed effort. Who better to do this work than the authors? Fortunately, the funder of The Moral Economy Project concurred and additional funds for promotion and marketing were added to our budget.

One detail remained to be approved—cover design. After several rounds of email attachments for our consideration, we had another conference call with Johanna and agreed on the cover. The designer had gotten the message; the subtitle was displayed in only slightly smaller font than the title. I intervened on one more detail; put the names of the two lead authors on the cover and the rest of us on the title page. Putting all five authors on the cover would be a graphic mess. In addition, it would create the impression of a book written by a committee, which, from a marketing point of view, weakens its presentation.

Peter Brown and Geoffrey Garver were the lead authors and the final edit adhered to their blended voice. In addition, they both had significant professional standing. Peter was a professor in the School of Environment, the Department of Geography, and the Department of Natural Resource Sciences at McGill University and had published two books. Geoffrey Garver's legal work included being senior counsel in the Office of Enforcement and Compliance at the US Environmental Protection Agency and a senior official at the North American Commission for Environmental Cooperation with respect to the North American Free Trade Agreement. He was a lecturer in environmental law and governance at several universities in Quebec. My suggestion was agreed to and *Right Relationship* went to print with an endorsement by Jimmy Carter on the front cover and by Gus Speth, Steven Rockefeller, and Elizabeth Dowdeswell on the back cover. Inside the front cover it carried four pages of ringing endorsements from Richard Norgaard, Herman Daly, Maurice Strong, Curt Meine, John Ehrenfeld, David Orr, Peter Barnes, Nina Leopold, and Sheila Abed, among others. Tom Lovejoy, founder of the PBS documentary series *Nature*, wrote the Foreword. Peter Brown was well connected in the world of ecological economics, environmental activism, and public policy and he drew on his connections for these endorsements. All five authors appear on the title page and are fully credited at the back of the book.

Johanna offered guidance on how to proceed with promotion and marketing. Our budget allowed us to engage a promotion agency and we spent the next year (2010) doing media interviews, making in-person presentations at various conferences and gatherings across the US and Canada, and soliciting reviews on behalf of *Right Relationship*. It's difficult to know how much these conventional promotion efforts contributed to the sales and circulation of the book. B-K initially printed 7500 copies. This is not a big number, but respectable for a book of this type. They eventually did a second printing and the book remains in print. We do know it was picked up by a number of study groups, was used in Poland as a text in an English learning class, and taken to Mozambique to be added to a college library. An enthusiastic Russian scholar told us he planned to translate it, but we have not had that confirmed.

One of the most touching appreciations we received was from a young woman at the annual gathering of the New York Yearly Meeting of the Religious Society of Friends (Quakers). After Geoff Garver and I completed our presentation, she stood up and thanked us for writing such a positive and helpful book. She said she had been struggling with whether or not to have children and our book had made her more hopeful about the future.

My second step into book publishing continued with Quaker Institute for the Future as we developed a series of short Focus Books that report on the research and analysis of QIF's collaborative working groups and, in some cases, the work of individual authors. QIF Board member Judy Lumb, already a publisher of natural history books in Belize, took on the editorial management of the Focus Book project with my assistance. To date, we have published twelve Focus Books with several more in process.[28]

And finally, my full immersion in book publishing has come with the late-in-life family project of developing Chapel Street

---

28   See https://quakerinstitute.org/books/

Editions (CSE), which brings me to my last story about working in the commonwealth of books.

• • •

A publishing venture devoted to the literature of place became a reality when Brendan, our son, returned to New Brunswick. With his expertise in graphic design and his command of digital technology, he is the Creative Director and Production Manager of CSE. With Ellen and I handling editing and office management, CSE was up and running in 2014. Our first publication was a book of poetry by an elderly friend, Hendrien Kippers, who lived near the city of Saint John on the Bay of Fundy.

She had composed a series of poems in which she gave voice to the heritage of the farmhouse and the land around it where she lived for many years. She had also written poems on city life in Saint John and on the constant and overarching presence of the ocean-like Bay of Fundy. We added these to the manuscript, which helped create a fully rounded expression of a sense of place. She had been writing for years and was now in her 80s. *Songs of the Ancestral Home* was her first book. She was well pleased and it was a fitting start for Chapel Street Editions.

We also began with the intent of republishing the books of George Frederick Clarke (1883-1974), a New Brunswick writer whose body of work exemplified the blend of natural history and cultural heritage that CSE was created to promote. Clarke started writing stories when he was twelve and never stopped. He grew up to be a dentist by trade but was always a writer by vocation. His New Brunswick contemporaries, Charles G. D. Roberts and Bliss Carman—writers who had achieved a degree of national and international recognition—told him he had to get to New York or London as they had if he hoped to make it in the literary world. Clarke declined. He loved where he lived and wanted to write about what he loved. He stayed home in Woodstock and eventually became one of New Brunswick's most esteemed writers.

Early on he wrote and published short stories in Canadian and American magazines of the day. He then wrote and published several novels, including three for young readers. Almost all of this work was set in New Brunswick and drew on his knowledge of its history and culture. But it was when he started writing about his other vocation—salmon fishing and life on the great rivers of New Brunswick—that two of his books garnered international recognition. *Six Salmon Rivers* and *Song of the Reel* are treasured classics within the salmon fishing communities of North America and Europe.

Clarke was also New Brunswick's first archaeologist. Although a self-taught amateur, he was a systematic explorer of ancient Indigenous settlement areas on the St. John (Wolastoq), Tobique, and Miramichi rivers. He collected and catalogued thousands of stone tools. His last book—*Someone Before Us: Buried History in Central New Brunswick*—is a comprehensive memoir of his pioneering archaeological work.

In addition, Mary Bernard, the Clarke family archivist, had completed a major biography of George Frederick Clarke, who was her grandfather, and was looking for a publisher. Thus was born the George Frederick Clarke Project with Mary Bernard, a published novelist, serving as the supervising editor for the republication of his books. We started with the simultaneous publication of three books: *The Last Romantic: The Life of George Frederick Clarke, Master Storyteller of New Brunswick* (Mary Bernard's biography), *Six Salmon Rivers,* and *The Ghost of Nackawick Portage: The Collected Short Stories of George Frederick Clarke*.

None of Clarke's short stories had been previously gathered for book publication and *The Ghost of Nackawick Portage* has been a hit. We included the original illustrations commissioned for magazine publication, which gives the book a vintage touch. At nearly five hundred pages and $35 it has been a surprising bestseller for CSE. We have now republished eight of Clarke's fourteen books and the project has helped anchor Chapel Street Editions in the literature of place.

In a similar way, the Tappan Adney Project has engaged CSE's commitment to the natural history and cultural heritage of our home region. Tappan Adney (1868-1950) travelled from New York

City to Woodstock, New Brunswick, in 1887 on a summer holiday at the age of eighteen. He was already an accomplished artist and a budding ornithologist. He was on track to enter Columbia University in the fall but stayed in NB for a year and a half. His encounter with the wilderness environment of the region and the Indigenous culture of the Wolastoqey people (at that time called Maliseet by the Europeans settlers) changed his life and ushered him into a vocation of ethnography, linguistic research, cultural preservation, and natural history journalism. He spent the next decade back and forth between New Brunswick and New York where he became a natural history journalist and public lecturer on Indigenous culture and wilderness adventure.

In particular, he was captivated by the fact that Indigenous craftsmen could simply walk into the forest, collect all the materials needed, and with a few simple tools build birchbark canoes. He apprenticed with a Wolastoqey canoe builder and mastered the craft. At the same time, he recorded every detail of the construction process in precise language and with detailed drawings. Adney was working with the last of the elderly canoe builders. His recording of their work and his mastery of the craft made him the man that saved the birchbark canoe.

In addition, he continued over the next several decades to research and build one-fifth scale models of the various bark canoes and skin boats that had been created and commonly used by all the Indigenous cultural groups across the continent. His book—*The Bark Canoes and Skin Boats of North America*—has become the workbench bible of all the birchbark canoe builders once again producing this heritage watercraft of elegant design and surpassing beauty.

Woodstock, New Brunswick was the origin and continuing epicentre of this ethnographic project. Our regional heritage organization, Carleton County Historical Society, maintains a museum in which a room is devoted to the Tappan Adney story. This story includes his pioneering linguistic research and the compilation of the first Wolastoqey dictionary, as well as his lifelong defense of Indigenous rights in dealing with the Canadian government.

Tappan Adney was the researcher who discovered the 1725 Peace and Friendship Treaty that proves the Indigenous peoples of the Maritime Region of Canada never ceded their land and resources to the European invaders and settlers. This discovery was of fundamental legal importance and forms the basis of land and access to resource claims even now on the frontline of nation-to-nation negotiations in our region of Canada.

With all this and even more that makes up the Tappan Adney story, the Carleton County Historical Society (CCHS) and the Town Council of Woodstock asked Chapel Street Editions to produce a short book that could be used to reach a wider audience about the significance of Adney's life and accomplishments. A full biography of Tappan Adney had been initiated in the early 1980s by James Wheaton, the husband of his granddaughter—Joan Adney Dragon. Unfortunately, he died before completing the manuscript, as did his co-author, Ted Behne. The project stalled and it was uncertain if the manuscript would ever be completed and published.

As it happens, I was thoroughly familiar with the Tappan Adney story, having first seen *The Bark Canoes and Skin Boats of North America* in 1968, four years after it was first published by the Smithsonian Institution. A colleague of mine at Friends World College had it open on his table as he and a group of students laid out their plans to build five canoes for an expedition from Long Island Sound through the East River into the Hudson and north into Canada. They built fibreglass canoes but the Adney book was their inspiration for design. In addition, we had become good friends with Joan Adney Dragon, Tappan Adney's granddaughter, who had a cottage at Skiff Lake in New Brunswick near Woodstock.

In 2017, with the encouragement of John Thompson, President of CCHS, and his wife, Lois, and with assistance of Adney researcher Daryl Hunter, I wrote *Tappan Adney and the Heritage of the St. John River Valley*. It was published by Chapel Street Editions and has become our best selling title. The unfinished manuscript of the biography eventually came to me for completion and publication by Chapel Street Editions. Thus began a three-year project parallel to the other publishing work CSE was doing at the same time. I extensively rewrote the manuscript, completed the missing parts, and relied on two additional authors—Daryl Hunter and Nicholas Smith—to contribute chapters on aspects of Adney's career that they had thoroughly researched. I then served as general editor for putting the whole book together, which was co-published by Chapel Street Editions and Goose Lane Editions in October 2024. *Tappen Adney: From Birchbark Canoes to Indigenous Rights* is a flagship book in CSE's mission of cultural heritage and natural history publishing.

In 2017 we also published a debut novel by Indigenous writer Peter J. Clair. *Taapoategl & Pallet: A Mi'kmaq Journey of Loss and Survival* was the winner of the 2018 New Brunswick Book Award for fiction. It has been widely recognized as a significant contribution to Indigenous literature and has been regularly adopted for reading in high school and college classes. We had long known Peter Clair as a superior craftsman in the art of split-ash basket making, which, from time to time, he brought to the Woodstock Farm and Craft Market. When he presented me with the manuscript of his novel, we set out together on the journey to publication. The reception of Peter's book is a benchmark for CSE in our promotion of the literature of place.

In 2019 CSE published a collection of short essays by Ken Homer that he wrote and recorded for broadcast on CBC radio over several decades. These essays, taken together, are a perfect blend of natural history observation and the celebration of cultural heritage. Although the reflections often draw on the larger scope of history and culture, his essays are anchored in the landscape and common life of the St. John River Valley. Ken had been a broadcast journalist with CBC radio and television. His voice was well known and his radio essays had a devoted following of listeners.

The Homer book, *Walks with a Three-Legged Cat & Other Observations*, was created by Stuart and Ross Kinney, a father and son team devoted to the history and culture of our region. They engaged a local artist, Michael McEwing, to create four full-page paintings to illustrate the seasons around which the essays are organized, and to make a woodblock print for the cover. Stephen Homer, son of Ken and Dees Homer, wrote a substantial memoir of his parents, illustrated with photographs, which makes a fitting Afterword. To achieve the best quality production, we had the book printed on 70 lb. paper. It's altogether a beautiful book and exemplary of the literature of place which is CSE's forte.

Stuart and Ross Kinney are now preparing another book for CSE publication. They are transcribing Ken Homer's interviews with Peter Paul, a Wolastoqey elder who was Tappan Adney's principal linguistic informant and a friend and associate of George Frederick Clarke.

As of spring 2025, Chapel Street Editions has published 51 books and has a full schedule of titles in process for many seasons to come.[29] CSE is incorporated as a non-profit cultural heritage and natural history publishing company. We are devoted to publishing New Brunswick writers who are telling New Brunswick stories. We are committed to advancing the appreciation and preservation of our region's natural environment and the cultural heritage of both Indigenous and settler communities. We believe that when people come to love the place where they live they will do all they can to preserve and enhance its ecological and social integrity.

This may seem a faint hope given the crushing pressures of the market economy for the extractive exploitation of natural resources and its erosion of fundamental community relationships. But there is evidence that attitudes are changing and the preservation of healthy forests, rivers and lakes, farmland, marine environments, and human communities is commanding the attention and commitment of an increasing number of people, especially young people.

Everyone who is paying attention knows the climate change crisis is planetary and must be addressed by public policy and environmental governance that stretches from local to national to global. But for most of us, where we live is the place we can

---

29   See www.chapelstreeteditions.com

engage with community and do the kind of work that adds a nurturing contribution to a secure, equitable, and sustainable way of life. With all this in mind, we see a publishing company devoted to the literature of place and making a contribution to cultural vitality and environmental integrity as a mission worth pursuing.

The mission of Chapel Street Editions engages cultural heritage in three dimensions—past, present, and future. Heritage work is usually thought of as preserving the knowledge, literature, arts, and crafts that come to us from the past, and this is as it should be. But cultural heritage is also continually unfolding in the present, adding to our means of social and environmental understanding, and, at its best, providing guidance for navigating into the future. This is the context in which CSE publishes the poetry, novels, and essays of current New Brunswick writers, as well as reprinting notable books from the past. We stand at the juncture of the present looking back at what should be preserved and looking ahead at what's coming up that will make a valuable, ongoing contribution to the literature of place.

This is a small niche in the panorama of forces and influences shaping and driving contemporary life, but it is a niche in which imagination and spirit are at work and often emerge in surprising and powerful ways. It is a niche in which even a small publisher can make a contribution to the great legacy of the commonwealth of books, a legacy that holds up a vast mirror in which we see and come to understand, at least in some partial way, the glories and agonies of the human story, and now, the fundamental crisis of the human-earth relationship.

Among the tipping points the human story has now reached, is a turn from the question "who are we" to the question "where are we." It is only with the terrain of earth fully in focus and the commonwealth of life fully in mind in a new and comprehensive way that our story may come to be told in terms of a mutually enhancing human-earth relationship. In that turning, the literature of place can have a leavening and enlightening effect. This is my faith and vocational summation as a long-time worker in the commonwealth of books.

Acknowledgements

In addition to the people mentioned in this memoir who played key roles at various points in my vocational life, this story rests in the companionship of Ellen and the way we have worked together in making major life decisions for the past sixty-seven years. Antoine de Saint-Exupéry wisely said that love is not so much looking at each other, as it is looking together in the same direction. And with our sons, Eric and Brendan, the sense of family solidarity that has accompanied all these years is a gift beyond measure.

Jay Bach, Brendan's child and our grandchild, took on the task of copyediting and proofreading, for which I am most grateful.

With the innate skill of a border collie rounding up a flock of sheep, Dan Traister corralled errant punctuation, technical glitches, grammatical infelicities, and a few outright errors that came to his attention. A deep bow of gratitude to Dan for generously helping polish the text of this book.

About the Author

Keith Helmuth grew up with a mother who read to her children—*A Child's Garden of Verses* by Robert Louis Stevenson, for example, and *The Yearling* by Marjorie Kinnan Rawlings, a book she loved and read aloud to her whole family gathered for repeated winter evenings at the dining room table after supper. He learned to read by picking up the adventure novels his older brother and sister brought home from the bookmobile service that made regular stops at their school in Aurora, Ohio—*Shadow in the Pines* by Stephen W. Meader and *Spirit of the Border* by Zane Grey, for example.

The opportunity for employment in the book business while still at university, led to a multi-faceted vocation: bookseller, bookstore manager, college librarian, college teacher, editor, and publisher, in addition to being a community development activist, small-scale farmer and market gardener.

Keith Helmuth was the delegate representing the Religious Society of Friends (Quakers) in Canada to the 1990 World Council of Churches' Convocation on Justice, Peace, and the Integrity of Creation in Seoul, Korea, where he served as a consultant to the drafting committee for the Convocation's final report. In 2003, he was instrumental in founding Quaker Institute for the Future.

He lives in Woodstock, New Brunswick, where he and his wife, Ellen, maintain a big garden and a small greenhouse.

Bookselling is a cultural and political expression, an expression of progressive change, of challenge to oppressive authority, of a search for a community of values which can act as an underpinning of a better world. The true profit in bookselling is the social profit; the bottom line, the measure of the impact of the books on the community.

David Schwartz (1927-2009)
Harry W. Schwartz Bookshop
Milwaukee, Wisconsin